Leading Change in th

Leading Change in the Early Years

Principles and Practice

Jillian Rodd

Mc
Graw
Hill
Education Open University Press

Open University Press
McGraw-Hill Education
McGraw-Hill House
Shoppenhangers Road
Maidenhead
Berkshire
England
SL6 2QL

email: enquiries@openup.co.uk
world wide web: www.openup.co.uk

and Two Penn Plaza, New York, NY 10121-2289, USA

First published 2015

A catalogue record of this book is available from the British Library

ISBN-13: 978-0-335-26370-7
ISBN-10: 0-335-26370-4
eISBN: 978-0-335-26371-4

Library of Congress Cataloging-in-Publication Data
CIP data applied for

Typeset by Aptara, Inc

Praise for this book

"This is a powerful text that utilises the voices of early years leaders to clearly articulate the challenges of leading change and demonstrate how the sector is rising to that challenge. It is, therefore, an excellent and vital resource for all working in the early years sector and comes at absolutely the right time as the pace of change in the sector continues to be fast flowing. This book comprehensively and accessibly draws together theory and practice enabling a thorough exploration of the subtle nuances within current debates as to the interrelationship and interaction of leadership and change. The closing thoughts at the end of each chapter are inspired; not simply a summary of the chapter, but an opportunity to underline the importance of key issues. The constructive and helpful strategies offered throughout the text give considerable support for those charged with leading change in the early years sector and, consequently, should be on the bookshelf of every early years setting."

Dr Caroline Leeson, Associate Professor of Early Childhood Studies,
Plymouth University, UK

"In a constantly changing world strong leadership and change management skills become of paramount importance and there is an increasing expectation that early years professionals are able to negotiate these domains. This text draws on research evidence and case studies from practice to support those dealing with change on a daily basis. By encouraging early years professionals to draw on their skills of leadership and interpersonal relationships, Jillian provides clear strategies to enact change. This is a 'must have' book for all those working in the Early Years."

Nikki Fairchild, Early Years Initial Teacher Training Programme
Coordinator, University of Chichester, UK

"At a time when early years practitioners everywhere are feeling pressure to respond to the children's policy agenda, this accessible guide offers support in implementing and sustaining change. Underpinned by theoretical models, Rodd explores the relationship between leadership and quality and identifies the dynamics of change within the processes of leadership. The text is complemented by comments from a wide of practitioners illustrating how professionals in different contexts experience and respond to the complexity of change."

Rory McDowall Clark, Senior Lecturer in Early Childhood, Worcester University, UK

"Jillian Rodd gives a contemporary view of leadership and change incorporating the latest research from the early years sector. Practitioner voices are evident throughout the book and bring the text to life, helping to contextualise theory explained in the chapters to real issues practitioners encounter in everyday practice. The book provides insight to the complexities of leadership and change, essential understanding for both early years students and practitioners."

Natalie Canning, Lecturer in Education - Early Years, The Open University

"This latest book from Jillian Rodd is timely as early childhood services continue to respond to the demands of policy and funding changes arising from continuing government interest in the early years. Another important application lies in responding to complexity arising from diverse communities and the challenges of improving and developing pedagogy and curriculum to enhance each child's learning and wellbeing. Currently there is little available that specifically addresses change in the early years. 'Leading change in the early years' progressively develops an argument that change is complex and multi-faceted, conceptualising change as encompassing quality improvement as a core function of early years services rather than as a special event to be managed. The role of leadership is presented as embedded within change where multiple leaders have responsibilities to contribute to change through building professional relationships that support collective endeavours within services.

In recognising the complexity of change the work draws on current research offering comprehensive coverage of the issues and significant factors associated with change, including the importance of establishing and nurturing a culture of learning within a service.

This latest work is very accessible and will be invaluable for existing early childhood leaders, aspiring leaders and tertiary students. I have no doubt this book will be valued as a companion to the acclaimed Leadership in Early Childhood now in the 4th edition."

Kaye Colmer, CEO Gowrie SA

"Change is the big 'c' word in contemporary educational environments. Information overload, turbulence and complexity characterise our everyday practice and our paths up ahead. The inevitability of change means we must be prepared and can be proactive in responding to external drivers, as well as in initiating reform. Most of all we must be willing to learn and to grow in our thinking. In this book, Jillian Rodd, a pioneer leadership researcher is once again, on the front foot, engaging early childhood readers with inquiry, insights and innovation. Rodd's approach to leading change makes it possible to embrace challenges as opportunities. This book is a 'must read' for intentional leaders seeking practical strategies for the everyday realities of early childhood settings."

ManjulaWaniganayake (PhD), Associate Professor at the Institute of Early Childhood, Macquarie University, Australia

Contents

Preface   xiii

Acknowledgements   xvii

Introduction   1

1 Change in early years provision   11
  Understanding change   12
  Theoretical perspectives of change   14
  Dimensions of change   14
  Process and models of change   18
  The process of change as a cycle of learning   22
  Factors that hinder and help the implementation of change   24
  Closing thoughts   25

2 Authentic leadership and change   27
  Quality improvement through competent leadership   30
  The power of leadership presence   35
  Leadership skills for making change happen   37
  Leadership roles for addressing change initiatives   39
  Closing thoughts   43

3 Leadership: The fuel driving quality improvement   45
  The relationship between leadership and quality   45
  Differentiating leadership from management   47
  The contribution of leadership to effecting change   49
  The impact of complexity on leading change for improvement   50
  A model for leading complex change   54
  Closing thoughts   59

4 Interpersonal relationships:
the foundations for effecting change   61

The role of trust in developing professional relationships   62

Professional interpersonal relationships in early
years settings   64

Key interpersonal skills for leading change   69

Issues affecting interpersonal relationships in early
years settings   71

Key skills for interpersonal competence in early
years settings   72

Closing thoughts   74

5 Effecting change through interpersonal communication   75

Communicating and listening: essential skills for
effecting change   77

Emotional intelligence and leading change   83

Roadblocks to effective communication in early
years settings   84

Communicating the vision for change   88

Closing thoughts   90

6 From reactive opposition to proactive receptivity
to change   91

The phenomena of opposition and resistance   91

Moving from shock to adjustment   95

Reducing stress in times of change   96

Common reactions to conflict about change   97

Strategies for channelling opposition into commitment   99

Encouraging proactive receptivity to change   104

Closing thoughts   106

7 Effecting change through collective endeavour   107

Benefits of collective leadership   108

Fostering collective commitment through
change champions   111

The power of collaborative teams in the change process   115

Closing thoughts   119

8 Sustaining change in a culture of learning   **121**

    The role of learning in change   123

    Early years settings as learning organizations   124

    Building a culture of learning and thinking   129

    Learning, leadership and change   132

    Learning and the development of capacity for
    change leadership   133

    Closing thoughts   136

9 Aide-memoire for leading change in the early years   **137**

References   141
Author Index   148
Subject Index   150

Preface

As the structure and content of this book were evolving, a colleague's comment compared the quest for quality improvement to ' . . . winds of change that sweep away the old and blow in the new'. This comment focused my thinking about the relationship between change and leadership. For me, leadership is a sail that uses the unpredictable winds of change encountered in the early years sector to chart a clear direction. Competent leadership prevents early years practitioners and settings from foundering through lack of wind or momentum, and from capsizing when battered by powerful forces that gust from different directions. Leadership is both a reliable rudder that steers the way and a stalwart anchor that keeps the sector from drifting and foundering as early years practitioners harness winds of change for improvement and reform.

This book builds on the general principles and practice of leadership by focusing on the type of expertise needed for leading the reform and change agendas that currently challenge the early years sector. Early years professionals who work in a diverse range of settings are expected to implement a range of government mandated directives, as well as professionally endorsed changes aimed at raising the quality of current provision. The ease and success with which mandated directives to improve quality are implemented within early years settings rests upon competent leadership of change, that is, knowledge, understanding and expertise in encouraging, supporting and working with everyone concerned with implementing and sustaining change.

This resource aims to unpick the principles, processes and practice of effecting change and offers early years professionals a practical guide to important elements relevant for meeting the current political agenda for quality improvement and the professional challenge of effecting responsible change.

The key content included in this resource covers:

- the link between competent leadership and successful change;
- selected dimensions, models and processes of change;
- leadership skills for effecting change within a range of roles and responsibilities;

- the contribution of trust, professional relationships and professional skills in making change happen;
- strategies for reducing reluctance and resistance, and for building receptivity to and readiness for change;
- the contribution of change champions, early adopters, teams and partnerships to enhancing willingness to engage with change;
- the role of a culture of learning in developing positive attitudes, approaches and commitment to change.

The material presented in this book is underpinned by relevant theoretical principles from the domains of psychology, sociology, education and business, which have been drawn together, interpreted for and applied to early years contexts. While some may argue that the early years sector is unique, unlike any other sector and workplace and, consequently, the contribution of theory, models and practice grounded in other disciplines has limited benefit, the changing perceptions, expectations and nature of early years provision (for example, multi-disciplinary teams, larger integrated centres, multi-agency provision and financial accountability) mean that it has more in common with other organizational types, structures and sectors than perhaps previously acknowledged. Indeed, Dunlop (2012) argues that if early years leadership is to be appropriate and competent for the diversity of provision, it has to draw on wider theoretical disciplines. The *CoRe Final Report* (Urban et al. 2011) comments that cross-disciplinary knowledge can only benefit the sector. The perspectives of other disciplines offer a basis for reflection, analysis, comparison, evaluation and innovative thinking and are the foundations for stimulating understanding, finding new possibilities for and improving workplace culture and practice in early years provision.

Early years provision functions within a global community (Rodd 2013b) and early years professionals have access to a range of literature about international provision (for example, Georgeson and Payler 2013), and therefore to the varied terminology used in different countries to describe both early years settings and those working in them (Oberhuemer et al. 2010). In addition, ongoing changes to early years qualifications (for example, the range of diplomas, higher education certificates, foundation degrees, ordinary, honours and higher degrees), work-based pathways to basic and higher qualifications and formally designated positions of leadership responsibility (for example, graduate leader) and roles (for example, early years teachers as change agents), mean that current nomenclature is increasingly varied.

Given that language can be ambiguous, confusing and potentially divisive, it is essential to define the terms used here to refer to those enacting significant leadership roles and responsibilities in early years settings, and those for whom leadership is a newer and evolving role and responsibility.

In this book, the generic and familiar terms of 'early years professional' and 'early years practitioner' refer to the women and men who are employed in a multiplicity of roles in the present range of early education and care settings. These blanket terms refer to those whose day-to-day responsibility is more typically focused on face-to-face interaction with young children but who, whether or not they hold formal positions of authority, instigate and effect both small and significant changes within early years settings. Regardless of title or role, they are usually expected to fulfil or hold some administrative responsibilities.

Those early years professionals with accredited qualified teacher status (QTS) may be referred to as nursery, kindergarten or pre-school teachers, Foundation Stage coordinators or pedagogical leaders or coordinators. Those holding various childcare qualifications may be referred to as early years teachers (non QTS), team or room leaders, early years or childcare educators, childcare workers and, less frequently, nursery or childcare nurses.

At times, the broad term 'leader' is used to refer to those who hold designated positions of leadership responsibility, and who typically enact administrative, management, supervisory and executive responsibilities within an early years setting. Some 'leaders' may combine leadership roles and responsibilities with child-focused day-to-day work in education and care settings. They may be referred to as head teachers, directors, coordinators or managers. In private or 'for profit' provision, they may be owners or licensees, though these people may not hold recognized early years or other relevant qualifications.

A key and underlying theme throughout the content of this book is the recognition of the right and responsibility of every early years professional to access and enact leadership regardless of position, qualifications and experience. The phrase 'those leading change' recognizes this professional value. However, it is important to acknowledge that different roles often have different foci and emphases within early years settings.

The term 'setting' refers to the range of provision or services that are offered to young children and families, including nursery and primary schools, daycare, childcare and nursery centres, kindergartens and preschools, home-based provision including family daycare and childminding, and age-integrated extended provision including out of school hours provision (for example, before school, after school and holiday provision).

Acknowledgements

The impetus for this book stemmed from interaction with early childhood professionals in England and Australia who presently are responding to diverse pressures for complex change. Many of the concepts and practices associated with leading change in early years provision have been illustrated and brought to life by their reflections, remarks and insights during recent professional development training opportunities.

I am indebted to those early years professionals whose generosity in sharing their thoughts, hopes, doubts and experiences will benefit others in the pursuit of excellence in these changing times. Any insight about the nature of change and the attitudes, attributes and skills associated with the successful leadership of quality improvement through change in early years provision is a product of their collective experiences and understanding. They are the early years sector's true leaders of change.

I wish to acknowledge the assistance of and thank the many people at Open University Press who have supported my writing, especially Fiona Richman, senior commissioning editor.

My life and work continue to be sustained by my anchor, Gerry Gray, my beloved late husband, who remains my rock and guiding star and to whose memory I dedicate this book.

Introduction

Continuity gives us roots, change gives us branches,
letting us stretch and grow and reach new heights.
Pauline R. Kezer

Change is a constant, significant but unpredictable feature of modern life and work. As societies develop, they become more complicated. Consequently, the complexity of the range and pace of change that people have to cope with also increases. Change, whether simple or complex, small or large, creates significant challenges, problems and perhaps opportunities for many individuals, teams and organizations. However, the need to adapt can be very threatening for many of us. Yet, failure to meet the demands of changing social, political and economic environments always has a negative impact on the success and survival of all concerned.

He who rejects change is the architect of decay.
Harold Wilson

Change and the necessity to adapt have been prominent hallmarks of early years provision since its inception, with the past 50 years witnessing considerable transformation in the type, range, delivery and content of provision available to and for young children and their families. A report by Action for Children (2008) presented some interesting statistics relating to children's services policy, legislation and politics in the UK between 1987 and 2008. During those 21 years, over 400 different initiatives, strategies, funding streams, legislative acts and structural changes affecting children's services were identified. Over half came between 2002 and 2008, and three-quarters between 1998 and 2008, which indicates a steady acceleration in government initiatives for change. Likewise, 15 years ago, Kagan (1999) noted that the US early childhood education sector was experiencing pressure for change as a result of growth, increased attention from politicians, policy-makers, media, researchers and parents, and consequently opening new opportunities for leadership.

It is apparent that early years professionals in various countries experience considerable and constant pressure to implement many different initiatives and developments. The pressure for change creates a further challenge, that of equipping the workforce with appropriate competence to achieve government targets. However, perhaps because they have experienced years of chronic change and limited training and support, some early years practitioners report that they are weary and wary of embracing yet more demands for change. Achievement of the current reform agendas and government goals rests upon enhanced professional capacity to understand and respond to directives for change appropriately.

> Recently, one of my team told me that she has no problem with change, yet, in reality, she is the one who finds suggestions about even the smallest alteration to her routine difficult, . . . she finds it so hard to see the bigger picture and accept that, in today's climate, we all need to be flexible and learn to work differently.
>
> Manager, children's services

Nevertheless, despite their past history of change, most early years professionals show willingness to step up to the current challenges faced by the sector.

> We've been waiting a long time for the impetus to get us going, to motivate us to move to a higher level in our work with children. These proposals are just what we need, it's exciting because of the possibilities that might come up. I say, bring it on.
>
> Coordinator, pre-school centre

Informed early years professionals understand that change and quality improvement are inextricably linked (Reed and Canning 2012). While professional values compel them to implement initiatives that they believe will improve quality, many report that they would benefit from support to incorporate the additional work required to implement demands for change with their already considerable workload.

This book offers information about key principles and practices that underpin making change happen in early years provision, with the intention of encouraging those involved in, affected by and leading the processes of improvement, reform and change to become confidently receptive to change, ready for change and appropriately skilled to proactively address the need for change. Although the early years sector currently is responding to various mandated government directives, early years professionals must also come up with their own ideas about ways to improve quality. Practitioners tend to be receptive to and engage more with ideas that they have generated because these are often considered to be more relevant to day-to-day practice. In addition, they are reminded that they are not only receivers of directives concerning improvement and change (Moyles et al. 2014) but also instigators, moderators and guardians, responsible for ensuring that any changes in legislation, policies and regulations affecting early years practice are in the best interests of young children and families. In addition, it is no longer acceptable that only those who hold formal titles or positions feel sufficiently confident and authorized to lead change (O'Gorman and Hand 2013). Regardless of their role or its source, it is important that every early years professional believes that they can influence change for improvement.

Because current pre-service training curricula must include a broad range of content and skill development, few opportunities are available to introduce and explore some of the more complicated professional issues and responsibilities, such as leadership and its role in effecting change. It is only recently that the importance of leadership aspiration, potential and practice (in which the roles and responsibilities for change are a key element) have attracted professional interest compared to the long-standing focus on curriculum, pedagogy and management. In addition, the capabilities underpinning efficient management of early years settings are not sufficient for the expert leadership required to guide practitioners and settings through the demanding process of change. Leadership is not and has never been a subset of management; competent leadership entails a different orientation, philosophy, values, attitudes, attributes and sets of capabilities. While the majority of experienced early years practitioners may learn to become efficient managers, fewer display sophisticated understanding about the need for change in the early years and specific leadership skills relevant to making it happen.

In times of change, it is important to foster leadership aspiration, potential and capability in every early years professional, regardless of position, qualifications and experience, through ongoing engagement, participation, learning, collaboration, mentoring and networking. Although the range of skills required to confidently address change in early years provision may initially appear daunting, unravelling the roles, processes and skills required for change can help clarify where and how each practitioner might contribute to making change happen. In so doing, they will develop increasing confidence about and skill in responding to demands for change, which over time become the catalysts for improving quality in early years settings.

Early years provision currently is delivered in extremely complex and dynamic social and political contexts that have generated many of the significant external challenges experienced by today's early years professionals. As well as contending with internal professional challenges stemming from a diversity of values, expectations and ethics, early years provision must

Policy overload.

comply with mandated stipulations set out in national law, national and local regulations, professional and government standards of quality and a range of government frameworks, directives and initiatives.

Given today's focus on improvement, reform and change, it is essential that early years professionals acknowledge the centrality of change in the delivery of responsive, relevant, sustainable and quality provision for young children and their families. Contemporary early years provision in the twenty-first century currently is shaped by policies aimed at strengthening an increasingly diverse range of families, building the foundations for lifelong learning and equitable access to quality early education and care for all children. Only provision that addresses, evolves and adapts to demands, pressures and changes in the current social, political and economic climate will be relevant and sustainable. The fact that some qualified and experienced early years professionals remain insufficiently prepared to identify and respond to the challenge of effecting professionally responsible change needs to be addressed by all concerned.

In the current climate, early years professionals are experiencing high expectations regarding their capacity to make change happen in the face of sometimes unjustified criticism, increasing pressures and considerable challenge. Rarely are their daily efforts to improve practice and provision publicly acknowledged. Despite this, government, professional, community and consumer insistence on the delivery of a broader range of quality early years provision has been unrelenting, regardless of fiscal constraints and increasing accountability. With constant pressure for change, the knowledge and skills acquired during pre- and post-service training may be inadequate or even obsolete for coping with current and future expectations and demands. Early years professionals now need sophisticated knowledge and expertise to integrate various statutory and professional obligations into coherent, meaningful pedagogy and practice that support young children's early development and learning.

In addition, the work environment has changed. No longer can positional or formal leaders of early years settings dictate the path to be taken in response to demand for change. More recently, the responsibility for change has tended to be distributed throughout early years settings, and genuine leaders are drawn from, and can be observed in, every position within provision. These informal 'leaders' are those practitioners who share knowledge, engage commitment, draw on communal experience and wisdom, create options, solve problems, take and encourage collective responsibility and thereby help build an inclusive and collaborative workplace culture. The culture of an early years setting is a subtle feature that can be discerned from the expression of values and action in day-to-day work. Practitioners who hold, aspire to or enact leadership in early years provision appreciate the importance of building an encouraging culture that nurtures receptivity, readiness and responsivity to pressure for change.

The complicated changes experienced today by those committed to improvement in early years provision require sophisticated and flexible cognitive skills. The following quotes by Albert Einstein and Kurt Lewin (a pioneer in the study of change) are particularly insightful and relevant for this day and age.

The world as we have created it is a product of our thinking.
It cannot be changed without our thinking.
Albert Einstein

If you want to truly understand something, try changing it.
Kurt Lewin

Early years training courses typically focus on the acquisition of rational, logical and linear thinking skills for problem-solving. However, change rarely follows a single pathway; complexity usually involves multi-dimensional and unpredictable problems and issues. Consequently, those who hold or take up leadership roles in early years provision need to develop a range of personal attributes and cognitive skills that are responsive and adaptive to whatever outcomes emerge from planning and systematic action. Moreover, the current pressure for improvement and change in early years provision is experienced in workplace contexts that tend to be emotionally charged and consequently require high levels of emotional intelligence in all concerned. Given that change can be threatening (Fullan 2001), some early years practitioners' initial responses to pressure for change may be reactive and unproductive. The need to remain calm, focused and rational in the face of colleagues' anxiety, reluctance, opposition or resistance requires considerable skill in emotional intelligence, which can be a personal challenge for some change leaders.

The process of change typically incorporates ideas and goals focused on improvement, enhancement and advancement. Unfortunately, change, even that grounded in well thought out, planned and systematic action plans might not necessarily achieve such goals. Stakeholders (that is, anyone who has an interest in or is affected by something) hold perceptions about the process of change and potential outcomes. Whether stakeholders perceive change as an improvement or advancement depends on a range of factors, including the reasons for change and the type, scale and pace of change. Factors such as personal cost versus personal benefits, individual versus collaborative responsibility and relative value to those concerned, impact on perceptions about change. Many stakeholders willingly step up to the challenge of change, some may debate the extent to which any proposed change could result in improvement, while others may passively or actively obstruct efforts at implementation. How those charged with leading change react to individual concerns, uncertainties and anxieties influences how easily and smoothly change will be effected. Consequently, understanding the process of change is critical in helping leaders make appropriate choices about how best to support others through this undertaking.

> *Be the change that you wish to see in the world.*
> Mahatma Gandhi

The past decade has witnessed many countries initiate major and statutory policy and reform agendas aimed at improving the quality of early years education and care (OECD 2012). These changes are complex because they are based around broad goals relating to families, access, equity, employment, enhanced early educational outcomes and improved quality provision. Such complex changes require considerable systemic, structural and personal transformation in order to be successfully and sustainably implemented within provision.

The current climate of global economic adversity has brought further pressures for early years professionals who wish to rise to and respond to the demands posed by the need for change. Early years provision is frequently targeted for cost savings and reductions in funding initiatives, changes that are rarely driven by the welfare and best interests of young children and families. For example, in England (a country with some of the highest childcare fees and lowest paid childcare staff in western Europe), a recent government proposal suggested that childcare could be made more affordable for families and costs cut by reducing staff:child ratios in some settings. Fortunately, many early years professionals drew on considerable professional expertise and experience, and convinced politicians and government officials that any cuts to staffing ratios in childcare provision would seriously endanger quality and safety while not making any savings for families.

Early years professionals regularly demonstrate that they can successfully oppose, resist and defeat changes that do not meet professional values, guidelines and standards. However, some authors (Bass 2000; Dunlop 2008; Rose et al. 2011) argue that similar capability needs to be encouraged regarding proactive attitudes and abilities for identifying need, being receptive to, ready for and instigating changes that lead to improved early years provision.

It is evident that early years professionals in many countries are being called upon to respond to complicated change agendas that are highly politicized and fiscally challenging, with long-term timescales and demanding high levels of professional and personal commitment and expertise. While many agree that change is timely and called for, some express frustration and uncertainty about ability to respond without adequate resources to support the range, complexity and pace of change expected, especially when so many regularly contribute over and above the expectations and requirements of their position during the course of their daily work.

Example of resisting change pressure.

I thought that the documentation was reasonably clear until I tried to translate it into day-to-day practice. Then, it seemed I couldn't understand the point of it, where I was supposed to go, what I was supposed to do differently, how I could make it better. I felt an enormous surge of frustration, anger and resentment at the people who told us we had to do this. They don't seem to understand just how hard our work is already and just want to pile more and more on top. They should try it for a day! All I feel now is stress and strain with no time to do anything properly. And I'll be the one who is blamed for not doing my job better. Those people won't be criticized for making my work harder than it already is.

Childcare worker, early learning centre

Research (Dunlop 2008) indicates that the way in which early years professionals enact, personify and engage with leadership determines the quality of early years provision. The ability to be receptive to, respond to and lead others through the process of change is a core leadership responsibility that has a specific set of skills and competencies. Successful and sustainable change in early years provision only comes about through effective leadership (Rodd 2013a). Consequently, every early years practitioner must build understanding about, skill in and personal capacity for meeting the demands and challenges of change in the sector. Furthermore, practitioners' receptivity and capacity to respond will determine how smoothly, quickly and successfully any change is implemented and embedded.

Significant, sustainable changes in early years provision are influenced by what leaders think, say and do. Those who successfully champion change prepare, educate, persuade, support, question, challenge and engage all concerned. They appreciate that barriers to change can be real but sometimes they may exist only in people's minds, as outcomes of thinking styles, previous experiences and emotional reactions. Effective early years leaders work collaboratively with practitioners and teams to create a culture that is grounded in professional values, positive and high expectations, personal initiative, quality work and collective responsibility. Simultaneously, they build a supportive workplace culture (grounded in respect, trust, cooperation and community) that protects, encourages and empowers everybody during potentially stressful processes of change.

More than ever, early years professionals appreciate that change in the sector will continue to arise out of and operate in complex social, political and economic contexts. Many already acknowledge, accept and meet their responsibility for addressing the need for complex change in early years provision in professional and creative ways, and appreciate that only when professionals, families and communities work together collaboratively will the complex changes demanded of the sector regarding improvement be successfully implemented and sustained.

According to Rosabeth Moss Kantor (1999), those leading change need three critical and enduring capacities:

* imagination to innovate (that is, entertain new possibilities, create new concepts, identify fresh pathways forward);
* openness to collaborate (for example, willingness to build connections);
* professionalism to perform (that is, best practice).

These three capacities are foundation skills for becoming an effective leader of change and are the core competencies that maintain and promote recognition of the professional nature, development and significance of early years provision in the twenty-first century.

There is a vast body of literature devoted to organizational theory and practice of change. However, in much of the early years literature, change is subsumed under another topic – for example, Aubrey (2011), Lindon and Lindon (2011), McDowall Clark and Murray (2012), Miller et al. (2012), Rodd (2013a) and Kingdon and Gourd (2014) – with fewer authors, such as Reed and Canning (2012) focusing attention directly on the relationship between change and quality improvement in early years provision. Goodnow (Snow and Van Hemel 2008) contends that it is important for early years professionals to understand that they typically develop routine ways of doing things and come to think of such practice as normal or natural. Seldom do we think about or question our routine practice because we often find it uncomfortable to make changes. Given that approximately 70 per cent of all change initiatives fail (Aigner 2011), it is essential for early years professionals to appreciate that leadership practice cannot be taken for granted and that, in order to be beneficial in times of formidable change, it too may benefit from explicit scrutiny, questioning, reflection and modification. In the twenty-first century, early years professionals should initiate and drive change and not remain passengers driven by others' agendas.

An overview of the various changes expected of early years education and care provision in OECD (Organization for Economic Cooperation and Development) countries over the past decade (OECD 2012) identifies a number of specific challenges for leaders and practitioners. These include:

* defining and building consensus in relation to the laws, regulations, goals, mandatory standards and initiatives for provision within the range of educational sectors;
* aligning the regulations, goals and standards with other sectors and levels of education, family and community provision;
* communicating and elucidating the regulations, goals, standards and initiatives to relevant staff and stakeholders;
* engaging stakeholders with proposed changes;
* translating goals into action and professional practice;

- securing appropriate and sufficient resources to meet quality standards, including opportunities for professional staff development;
- adapting action and professional practice on the basis of local needs, expectations and constraints;
- implementing the regulations, standards and initiatives effectively;
- evaluating both the content and implementation processes.

Early years leaders who are charged with meeting the challenges of today's change agendas will find that personal and professional abilities and resources may be tested by such demanding and potentially stimulating tasks.

Closing thoughts

In many countries, the early years sector is experiencing considerable pressure for change and it can be tempting for leaders and practitioners to respond to pressing matters with short-term solutions, which may prove to be unsuccessful and ineffective in the long term. It is much harder to respond to immediate pressure and calls for change using careful analysis, systematic preparation, meticulous planning, methodical implementation and rigorous evaluation. Therefore, every early years professional should augment personal knowledge about and skill in effecting change. This book specifically addresses some of the critical issues, skills and practices that underpin effective leadership for implementing and sustaining the demanding changes to which early years professionals in many countries must respond.

1
CHANGE IN EARLY YEARS PROVISION

Change is the only constant. Nothing endures but change.
Heraclitus, Greek philosopher, 540–480 BC

This chapter explores:

▶ the concept of change;
▶ theories, dimensions, features and processes of change;
▶ differences between simple and complex change;
▶ steps in a cycle of change;
▶ change as a cycle of learning;
▶ factors that hinder or help the implementation of change.

Change is the process of making, becoming or causing something to be different. In early years provision, change is guided by inspiration and vision for quality improvement in practitioners who act to help people and settings transition from outmoded states to more appropriate and desirable states. Change in early years provision focuses on goals for improvement, enhancement or advancement in the quality of relationships, practice or services for children and families. Consequently, within early years provision, demand for change can become a catalyst for improvement (McDowall Clark 2012). Change can occur in individual practitioners at a personal level, for example to achieve a goal, self-improvement, to meet internal or external pressures, to control life and work, or to create a better future. Change also occurs in processes, structures, systems and workplaces, for example because of changes in external contexts and environments, pressures to respond or adapt to external influences, demands from external regulators, competition, new challenges, emerging opportunities and the desire to make a positive difference.

Change can come about because of dissatisfaction with the current situation and/or work practice. For example, the extent of lower-level workforce qualifications has driven the current directives concerning higher qualifications for early years practitioners. Ideally, change is motivated by a vision of better alternatives and the product of a coordinated effort of a group of stakeholders working together to achieve shared goals. To continue with the example, it is envisioned that practitioners who hold higher qualifications will provide better quality early education and care. Change can be brought about in attitudes, beliefs, behaviour, practice and understanding. It can refer to making something different by adapting, converting, improving or transforming what already exists; abandoning, replacing, exchanging or substituting the old with new; inventing or doing something new; connecting existing things to make something different and becoming different for the better in some way.

In the past, the early years sector in most western countries has successfully initiated and implemented many changes, including:

- advances in theory and practice of teaching and learning in care and education;
- collaborative teamwork and distributed leadership in provision;
- creation of a unique professional identity;
- development of a culture of learning;
- prioritization of specific ethical values in provision such as access, equity, diversity and inclusion;
- broadening and integration of provision;
- establishment of multi-disciplinary, multi-professional, multi-agency teams and partnership in provision for children and families;
- statutory requirements relating to qualifications and professional development for those who work with and for children and families;
- initiatives aimed at quality assurance and improvement.

Regardless of scope, form and early years context, each of these changes has depended on competent and authentic leadership along the often slow and difficult road of implementation and sustainability. Experience of change has shown that the more complex it is, the greater the need for skilled leadership. In this current climate of reform and change, it is essential that relevant government departments as well as all members of the early years sector acknowledge the importance of, invest in and secure competent leadership.

Understanding change

In the early years sector, the ability to influence and implement change is a core and critical function and responsibility of early years professionals. Ability to lead change is underpinned by knowledge, strategies, structures, people, procedures and technologies that are used to respond to pressures from external and internal forces. When leadership in early years provision is effective, those affected by any proposed change develop sufficient confidence to relinquish aspects of current practice and transition to new ways of working. An understanding of the reasons and benefits of change helps early years practitioners to accept, endorse and enact a new order or desired way of working.

Contemporary leadership in early years provision is a dynamic and holistic endeavour that demands personal capacity for vision, commitment, innovation, flexibility, shrewdness, decisiveness and action to ensure that provision and employees remain responsive, relevant, current and possibly even ahead of their time (Rodd 2013a). It also requires some degree of professional maturity, a quality that is independent of age and experience. Such attributes and capabilities drive and guide the energy and effort of early years practitioners and settings towards continuing improvement, innovation and transformation of provision for young children and families. Effective leadership of change requires early years leaders and practitioners to draw upon their insight, energy, determination, persistence, maturity and resilience to ensure that quality provision is sustained, improved and advanced.

Change is a natural, necessary and inevitable phenomenon and one of the few certainties in all aspects of life, including work. It has been a recurring theme in the early years sector for many decades and continues to be so (Kagan 1999). Change is the energy and driving force behind growth, development, improvement, advancement and fulfilment. Without change, both life and work would stagnate and show little sign of activity, direction, development or advancement. In addition, indications of deficiency, decline, deterioration, irrelevance, malfunction, degeneration, failure and atrophy would be increasingly obvious. Without change, individuals, teams and workplace culture quickly become bored, jaded, demotivated, apathetic, uninvolved and indifferent. Human beings need a certain amount of challenge to experience and display mastery, competence and self-fulfilment. Change, when led competently, can offer such opportunities.

Given that considerable change is experienced in day-to-day life, it is perplexing that the process of change presents as an unwelcome event for many people. Even when they appreciate and accept the need for and reasons behind change, many prefer to cling to the routine and familiar. Indeed, one of the realities of change is that it will be openly and/or covertly, actively and/or passively resisted by many of us.

According to Fullan (2001), change is always perceived as a threat, especially change that emanates from complexity and the unknown. In addition, change, especially complicated change, can generate uncertainty, confusion, anxiety, fear, stress and other negative emotions. Typically, responding to the demands of change calls for people to move out of their comfort zone, relinquish the known, familiar, routine and established, and accept, learn and adopt new, different, possibly challenging, attitudes, behaviours, practices and ways of working. This is why many of us benefit from support and encouragement when faced with demands for change.

Theoretical perspectives of change

Those who are competent leaders of change in early years settings use leadership and change theory to raise the quality of early years practice (Davis 2012). They tend to construct a personal conceptual framework that helps them understand and guide the process. Such theories are built upon ideological foundations grounded in assumptions about the nature of change, role of people and influence of the external context. Appreciation of different theoretical perspectives about change helps early years leaders and practitioners understand the driving forces behind change, that is, why change happens, how processes of change may unfold (for example, stages, scale, timing), what the likely outcomes might be, and ways of measuring and evaluating success.

Numerous theoretical perspectives about the basis and processes of organizational change are available in the literature (Van de Ven and Poole 1995; Kezar 2001). The foci of six major paradigms are summarized below.

- **Life cycle:** exploring processes of growth, maturity and decline in both individual change in human beings and systemic change in organizations.
- **Evolutionary:** exploring adaptive models, systems and chaos theories.
- **Dialectical:** exploring social interaction, values-driven and political models.
- **Teleological:** exploring rational planned change through problem-solving, action research and scientific measurement.
- **Social cognitive:** exploring how learners and team members make sense of and shape their view of change through interpretation and framing.
- **Cultural:** a blended approach (incorporating dialectical and social cognitive assumptions) examining change as a response to alterations in values and norms within social and cultural contexts.

Currently, evolutionary and teleological assumptions about change are popular, as well as multiple models that meld aspects from the above six approaches (for example, Senge's (2006) systems thinking and learning organization perspective). Because every theory of change has strengths and weaknesses, those who wish to lead or are responsible for making change happen in early years settings are advised to consider and assess which, if any, perspective offers the best fit for their particular style, needs and context. In early years settings, approaches that focus on social interaction, values, learning, planning and evaluation appear to be most appropriate for effecting change.

Dimensions of change

The study of change is not new. A considerable body of literature and applied research is available in various contexts, including business, health, social work and education. Effecting change in organizations (including early years provision), communities, cultures and societies is contingent upon authentic leadership which ensures that stakeholders (that is, interested parties) work together to enact and embed new behaviours, practices and systems. Change initiatives have a greater probability of failure where leadership is weak, directionless and unskilled (Kotter 2003).

In any organization, including early years settings, careful planning by those leading change is required to generate overall support and commitment to implementation. Change that is properly thought through and planned moves through a sequence of organized and structured transitions from initiation to embeddedness. Effective leadership of change must be in place in early years settings, formally and informally, before the start of any initiative; ideally, leadership responsibility will be accessible and genuinely distributed to practitioners through every facet, transition and stage of the change processes.

Effecting change is a complicated process. It happens through the interplay of interrelated constituent parts, with alterations in one constituent precipitating adjustment in others. Those leading change need to understand the interaction between the following elements:

- people (human resources);
- practices (work);
- culture (values, attitudes, ideas and customs); ══➤ culture.
- systems (vision, mission, goals, strategies and processes);
- technology (or tools).

Change is foremost a people process; it happens because people want it to happen, or not, as the case may be. Fortunately, some people thrive on change and actively pursue it. However, others may avoid, react against or resist change regardless of how it is presented or what it entails. Therefore, those who lead change in early years settings need to be aware of and address practitioners' habitual reactions when introducing it. Some practitioners initially may not understand why changes are required and consequently debate, challenge, oppose or resist them. The reasons underpinning any change need to be clear for those who may have to alter their role or day-to-day practice or who are otherwise affected. Happily, few members of the early years workforce are recalcitrant and obstructive in relation to implementing their professional or provision's collective vision. Nevertheless, change is unlikely to be successful without full commitment from the vast majority.

There are many types and degrees of change, all of which vary in scope and complexity. A range of factors determines the type and magnitude of change that is encountered in early years provision. Each factor will impact on how best to lead the process of change. For example, any change can be:

- simple or complicated;
- minor or major;
- positive or negative;
- expected or unexpected;
- easy or challenging;
- acute or chronic;
- comfortable or unpleasant;
- gradual or rapid;
- episodic or continual;
- voluntary or compulsory;
- necessary or optional;
- anticipated or unpredictable;
- timely or inopportune;
- clear or nebulous;

- incremental or radical;
- planned or opportunistic;
- programmed or crisis;
- controlled or chaotic;
- reactive or rational;
- emergent or obsolescent;
- traditional or progressive;
- uncreative or innovative;
- to preserve or to alter the status quo;
- a transition or transformation;
- and combinations of all of the above.

An analysis of the various factors that contribute to and define the parameters of change offers some insight into how best to lead it. In any change agenda, smaller, simpler, positive, planned and less emotional changes will be easier to implement; whereas major, complicated, compulsory, crisis and innovative changes are more likely to generate negative emotions and subsequently be more challenging to implement. The greater the complexity and the more elements that need to be changed, the more difficult the process is likely to be.

In relation to the current reform directives, the majority of early years leaders and practitioners accept them as timely, innovative and challenging; many use the phrase 'bring it on' to describe their attitudes to change. Fortunately, fewer practitioners view the directives from a negative perspective. Nonetheless, terms such as complicated, reactive, difficult, unnecessary, unfavourable and untimely have been used to describe what is expected and happening. Those leading change initiatives and agendas in early years provision may counterbalance any negativity with trust, respect, empathy, encouragement, confidence, enthusiasm and reassurance about the personal and professional benefits of embracing change.

> I've been looking forward to these proposed changes for quite a while. They are well overdue. Our team needed something, a positive reason, to spur us on to work towards achieving an even higher quality service than we already deliver. We are all excited about the future and developments. We think we can – and we will – rise to the challenges the government has set for us.
>
> Team leader, childcare centre

Complexity.

Although change varies in form, degree and scope, the intricacies of con-temporary society and its systems mean that many changes will be compli-cated rather than simple. Early years provision is part of a larger composite political, social and educational network and system where complex changes are the norm rather than the exception. Early years settings themselves are complicated workplaces with unique structures, and their own professional cultures and climates. Early years provision, historically and currently, func-tions within broad systems that expect positive and appropriate responsivity to ongoing and challenging demands for complex change.

Complex change can only be successful if every member of the early years workforce learns to question the status quo, and rises to the chal-lenge of reconceptualizing, approaching and performing professional roles, functions and responsibilities in different ways. Some early years practitioners report that, for them, this means working smarter not harder. Those who successfully lead change support early years professionals to adapt through the process by planning strategically and making sense of change by offering direction, ensuring orderly transitions and prog-ress, and where possible protecting colleagues from loss, humiliation and failure.

For these reasons, it is helpful if those leading change in the early years distinguish between change that is relatively simple and change that is com-plex, transformational and requiring higher-order cognitive, emotional and behavioural abilities. Successfully meeting the demands of complex change requires early years professionals to move out of their comfort zone into a learning zone where, supported by a workplace culture that values collabor-ative learning, they develop proactive receptivity and readiness to embrace change as a normal part of day-to-day responsibilities. However, the diffi-culty in pushing and pulling human beings out of their comfort zone should not be underestimated. Reluctance and resistance can be powerful forces and very damaging to attempts to modify what is familiar and comfortable. Table 1.1 illustrates the ways in which complex change differs from simple change on a range of key dimensions.

Complex change, such as demanded by the current reform directives, generally entails conflicting priorities, vague boundaries, multiple pathways, options and potential solutions, and ambiguous issues and problems. The sig-nificance of early years professionals' perceptions and definitions of change, level of commitment, as well as political, cultural and economic influences, should not be underestimated. Those who successfully lead change tend to adopt more holistic approaches to and sophisticated strategies for respond-ing to the challenge of complex change.

In summary, the complex changes that are associated with many of the current reform directives for improving early years provision are:

- multi-layered and multi-dimensional;
- unique situations or demands that continue to undergo transition;

Table 1.1 Simple vs complex change

Simple change	Complex change
More technical	More organic
Linear causal	Non-linear causal
Low dimension	High dimension
Predictable	Unpredictable
Familiar	Surprising
Replicable	Unique
Open to control	Open to influence
Incremental	Punctuated, radical

Source: adapted from Olsen and Eoyang (2001)

- open-ended with no final or specific end point – the future end point for quality improvement is unknown;
- open to multiple approaches and potential pathways forward;
- complicated by many critical and difficult factors that must be addressed;
- potentially meaningless or lacking sense for some practitioners, leading to frustration, friction, stress, resistance and obstruction;
- reliant on commitment and collaboration that grow out of supportive relationships, a culture of learning and expert leadership.

Process and models of change

Change, particularly within the early years sector, is a process that generally takes place over time: it does not come about through a single event and it does not result from one meeting or briefing. The process of change is seldom easy and rarely is it gradual, logical, sequential and controllable. However, it is achievable. Early years leaders and practitioners should never feel overwhelmed or disheartened about their ability to successfully implement any aspect of proposed change.

Typically, change takes place slowly through discrete stages distinguished by specific strategies and processes. Consequently, change happens through a series of achievable steps, each of which has a specific focus and concomitant leadership competencies, roles, tasks and responsibilities.

In the 1940s, Kurt Lewin (Cummings and Huse 1989) proposed a simple three-step model, which illuminates the basic processes involved in making change happen. This model dominated understanding and thinking about change for over half a century and although Lewin's theory has attracted criticism in recent times (Burnes 2004), this three-step teleological model continues to inform the leadership of change today. The three steps are as follows.

- **Unfreezing**, where the current equilibrium needs to be destabilized or 'unfrozen' before outdated attitudes, behaviour and practices can be discarded or unlearned and desired attitudes, behaviour and practices are successfully and routinely adopted. Schein (1988) argued that unfreezing relies on three processes: disconfirmation of the validity of the current state of affairs; the induction of survival anxiety; and creating psychological safety. Most importantly, before stakeholders can accept any changes and reject outmoded attitudes and practices, they must feel safe from loss, humiliation and failure. Stakeholders' receptivity to, preparation and readiness for change must be encouraged, stimulated and enhanced to help them to let go of the past and focus on the future. Any initial apathy, reluctance, resistance, opposition and barriers to change must be spotted and addressed. Leaders lay the groundwork for activating successful change initiatives in this stage.

- **Changing**, where systematic action plans identify and evaluate available options. This step highlights the importance of learning, risk-taking, creativity and reflection in the process of change. However, the complexity of the forces that contribute to and impact on change can make it very difficult to predict or identify specific outcomes. Because stakeholders may experience such uncertainty as lack of control, uncertainty and havoc, those leading change need to offer ongoing support for, motivation and confidence in people's ability to meet new demands and challenges. Learning and reflection are the means by which individuals and teams move from an unsatisfactory situation to more acceptable and improved circumstances. However, without feedback, recognition of and reward for progress and achievements, change could be short-lived. Those leading change need to be aware of the importance of the human and emotional aspects of implementing change.

- **Refreezing** is the final step where attention is focused on strengthening and embedding a new stability that ensures the changed attitudes and practices are assimilated, routinized and integrated into normal work repertoires, and subsequently become safe from a return to old ways. New attitudes and practices need to be relatively congruent with stakeholders' professional identity and workplace culture or they might be invalidated. Change only takes root when those leading it ensure that stakeholders' self-esteem and self-confidence remain intact and are enhanced.

According to Lewin, in order for change to occur, the forces that drive it must exceed the forces that restrain it. If these are balanced, there will be no change. Both internal and external forces drive change. Examples of internal forces relevant to early years provision include the need to increase efficiency, improve quality, remain financially viable and grow a professional culture that incorporates knowledge-sharing and learning. Examples of external forces include demand, cost, competition, government regulations and statutory obligations, political influences, ethical considerations, social values and technological changes. In order to initiate the unfreezing process, those leading change in early years provision must identify the forces that drive and motivate practitioners to embrace change, and act to lessen or eliminate those forces that reduce the probability of change taking place.

> The hardest aspect of getting change going in my setting has been the staff's unwillingness to give up what they know, to be open to new ways of working, and to try out new ideas. Once they try something and it works, they are more willing to try something else. It is just the first push to get them going, that's the hardest . . .
>
> Coordinator, childcare centre

In reality, early years provision operates in a far more complicated and less stable context than this model allows for. Change happens, but it takes place gradually over time. More often, it is a cyclical process similar to that of action research (McNiff and Whitehead 2009), where small improvements are made with each repetition of the cycle. It is unlikely that final refreezing and new stability will be achieved in one cycle; it is more likely that the last step of the cycle begins a new round of unfreezing and changing towards the targeted goals. Contemporary interpretation and application of Lewin's teleological and step model incorporates an additional preliminary stage of 'diagnosis' as summarized below.

- **Diagnosis:** analysing the current situation and identifying both the desired goals and targets and the problems and barriers faced in reaching them.
- **Unfreezing:** reducing the forces that maintain the status quo or that perpetuate unsatisfactory attitudes, behaviours or practices.
- **Changing:** planning and taking action to shift attitudes, behaviours and practices to the preferred state.
- **Refreezing:** stabilizing the new circumstances so that they become embedded as the norm.

In many documented models of change (Senior and Swales 2010), the stages and steps generally describe processes around stakeholders':

- awareness of the need to change;
- desire to participate and support the change;
- knowledge about how to change;
- ability to implement new skills and behaviours;
- reinforcement as motivation to keep the change in place.

Proschaska and DiClemente's life cycle stage model of change (1988; Health Promotion Unit 2007) outlines five stages, which are described as:

- **Pre-contemplation:** no intention to change due to a genuine lack of awareness or appreciation of existing need, dissatisfaction or problem. Stakeholders are not interested in change, cannot see the need and have no intention of doing anything differently.

- **Contemplation:** appreciation of an existing need to change (although some may still feign ignorance) but no commitment to action. Stakeholders generally acknowledge that there is a problem and a possible need for change. They begin to think about what they could do to make things better. Feigned ignorance is an indication of passive opposition and resistance to changing the status quo and must be addressed immediately.

- **Preparation:** committed intention to respond and take action. Stakeholders understand that change is going to happen and begin to prepare for it by gathering information, determining options, making plans, and reaffirming the need for and desire to change.

- **Action:** stakeholders learn, adapt and modify attitudes, beliefs, behaviour, practice and systems in order to respond to change directives. This is when people need support to help them integrate new beliefs and practices into their attitudinal and behavioural repertoires.

- **Maintenance:** stakeholders work to consolidate and embed changes to prevent relapse into old ways. Progress and achievements need to be recognized and celebrated to ensure the changes survive.

Although this model's focus is on personal change within individuals, the orientation of each of the stages offers insight into stakeholders' perceptions, emotions and potential barriers to progress and helps those leading change to understand what types of issues they need to address to help stakeholders successfully embed change in personal and professional repertoires.

The various models offer those leading change a structure for advancing the process. When faced with the challenge of responding to change directives, those leading change in early years settings may find Kotter's (2003) eight-step teleological model helpful.

- **Step 1: create a sense of urgency** around the need for change within the setting. A sense of gravity and necessity can help spark initial motivation.

- **Step 2: form a powerful coalition** though competent leadership. Gather the 'enthusiasts' together in an alliance focused on convincing others, engendering support for and building momentum around the need for change.

- **Step 3: create a vision** for change. Clear, compelling vision and strategies help everyone make sense of proposed change, and appreciate the need for, reasons behind and direction of change.

- **Step 4: communicate the vision** of change. Frequently talk about the 'big picture' and the benefits of change, openly and honestly address concerns and anxieties, become a role model for the attitudes, beliefs and practices that support change.

- **Step 5: remove obstacles** to change. Engage and empower practitioners, and increase the rate of progress towards realizing the vision, by overcoming or eliminating potential and existing barriers to embracing change.

- **Step 6: create short-term wins.** Success is a powerful motivator and can help counteract the voice of critics, detractors and negative thinkers. Celebrate and reward short-term and small successes and those who contribute towards goal achievement.

- **Step 7: build on the change.** Long-term change is grounded in aspiration for continuous improvement, not short-term gains. Focusing on short-term successes, especially before they are truly cemented as normal and routine, can diminish motivation over time.

- **Step 8: anchor the changes in workplace culture.** For any change to stick and embed in day-to-day practice, it has to become part of a setting's core values and culture at every level and with every practitioner.

Kotter (2011) argues that solid foundations need to be laid by those who lead change to ensure that any proposed change is understood, accepted, addressed, appropriately implemented and constantly maintained by everyone involved.

The process of change as a cycle of learning

If the process of change is understood as a cycle of learning, key steps can be identified that break it into small, understandable and achievable tasks for those who are novices as well as those who are more experienced in addressing proposed change. Most early years professionals will have encountered the well-documented cycle of action research and the learning process of professional reflection in training and professional development opportunities. The sequence of steps in the process of change is remarkably similar to that of action research and professional reflection on practice (Hopkins 2008; Costly et al. 2010). Consequently, many early years practitioners will be familiar with the following steps in the process of change.

1   Identify, define and agree on the issue or concern that could be improved. Create a shared inspirational vision. Communicate the need for change, situate it within a professional culture of learning (see Chapter 8), and evaluate preparedness for and readiness to change. Explain how the situation will look when changed.

2   Undertake a needs assessment to identify and prioritize factors that are relevant or may contribute to the need for change. Identify opportunities and impediments. Identify and motivate potential change champions and leadership partnerships (see Chapter 7).

3   Set specific goals and select appropriate strategies, decide what or who has to change and in what ways, who needs to be involved and sources of support, impediment and resistance (see Chapter 6).

4   Develop a feasible and achievable action plan that allocates tasks, responsibilities, people and other necessary resources, including a structure for regular reporting.

5   Implement and monitor action plans using agreed indicators, deliverables and timelines. Motivate ongoing commitment using change champions.

6   Analyse, evaluate and celebrate what has been achieved, make fine adjustments where necessary, identify what has been learned for future planning.

7   Start the next cycle based on what has been learned and identified priorities.

Those who successfully effect change in early years settings acknowledge the benefits of breaking complicated reform proposals into manageable, achievable and sequential steps that are part of a connected and integrated cycle. When complicated change is divided up into steps, sequences and stages, most early years practitioners feel more confident about their ability and empowered to make change happen. As a result, less resistance to the process is encountered. When small goals are reachable, small successes and even slight progress towards bigger goals can be celebrated. This process helps to reaffirm vision, and recognize and reward contributors and participants. Evident progress becomes further motivation and attracts remaining resisters, opening the way to embark on the next step or cycle.

Competent leaders of change in early years provision understand that successful implementation is accomplished by focusing on creating and building:

•   shared vision and values;
•   strategies for engaging, enlisting and empowering practitioners;

- clear and well-articulated goals, procedures and strategies that scaffold the process and monitor progress;
- sufficient human and relevant resources;
- change champions who promote shared ownership through commitment to collaborative action and collective responsibility;
- visible and confident leadership throughout settings that influences, guides, supports and mentors everyone through transitions to achievement.

Factors that hinder and help the implementation of change

Leading change is a demanding responsibility and, even with the most skilled leadership, the majority of change initiatives fail to take hold, fizzle out or fold (Beer and Nohria 2011). While no combination of critical factors can guarantee that change will happen, certain factors, including vision, communication, trust, commitment, motivation, teamwork and distributed leadership, are known to be key to successful outcomes; whereas reliance on management approaches, hierarchical authority, formal roles and rules, fixed procedures, rigid structures and inflexible workload parameters are known to act as impediments.

In addition, Garvin and Robardo (2011) identify six other factors that may hinder the successful implementation of change initiatives:

- a workplace culture dominated by risk-avoidance, criticism and habitual opposition;
- over-emphasis on the *what* – the content and ends, rather than the *why* – the reasons, and the *how* – the process and means;
- avoidance tactics by leaders or practitioners that deflect attention from unpalatable and challenging issues;
- deceptive displays of overt cooperation and consensus at meetings followed by covert debate, resistance and obstruction;
- over-analysis and micromanagement of proposals and action plans that results in muddled, ambivalent and inconsistent thinking and decision-making;
- ignoring, working around or delaying action on proposed changes.

Those who successfully lead change in early years settings appreciate that such dysfunctional strategies by others hamper and block the progress of change initiatives and must be addressed. They focus on communicating that current circumstances necessitate new ways of thinking and working, and are willing to work with, mentor and coach others to persuade them to accept and commit to shared responsibility for making change happen.

It is amazing, I can predict those team members who will automatically say no, those who will drag their feet and those who come up with extraneous arguments about why any ideas to respond to the framework won't work. It's not as if we can ignore it, we have to take it on board.

Director, early learning centre

Beer et al. (2011) suggest that leaders who encourage coordinated teamwork, expect high levels of commitment and facilitate the acquisition of new knowledge and competencies are more likely to gain team cooperation for effecting change. In addition, complex change initiatives will be successful when those leading change ensure that team members accept that greater effort and activity than normally expected are required, and that everyone involved needs to 'go the extra mile' and work outside, beyond and above existing job descriptions and responsibilities. Fortunately, most early years practitioners are familiar with and are willing to meet such expectations.

Macfarlane and Cartmel (Macfarlane et al. 2011) contend that successfully embedding any change into early years professional practice and settings is an outcome of:

- circularity, that is, collaborative, reciprocal learning spirals resulting from ongoing dialogue, conversation and debate;
- critical thinking, including analysis, reflection and integration of multiple perspectives to construct new understanding and ways of working;
- conflict resolution, that is, positive and constructive strategies for working through disagreements, resolving conflicts and moving to consensus;
- cementation, that is, consolidating, incorporating, grounding and securing new learning, thinking and ways of working into routine practice;
- culture, that is, a mindset and professional identity valuing and promoting lifelong learning, thinking, continuous development and improvement;
- continuity, a process of modification, adjustment, change and evolution that happens over time.

Those interested in leading change in early years settings are encouraged to become familiar with factors that impede and facilitate the process of change when addressing demand for reform and improvement.

Closing thoughts

Change occurs in individuals, organizations and societies, and change at any one of these levels will necessarily require change in the others. However, change in the early years sector rests on competent leadership, the key ingredient for the successful implementation and sustainability of current reform agendas. The process of change demands modification of practitioner attitudes and skills, as well as adjustments in policies, procedures, structures and systems. Because change is an inevitable, continuing process in life and work, every early years practitioner, regardless of position, qualifications or experience, needs to learn to approach it positively and confidently, and be supported by leaders who are encouraging, enthusiastic and confident about the team's ability to embrace change and effect professionally responsible quality improvement.

2

AUTHENTIC LEADERSHIP AND CHANGE

*If your actions inspire others to dream more, learn more,
do more and become more, you are a leader.*
John Quincy Adams

This chapter explores:

▶ leadership of change within early years provision;
▶ authentic leadership;
▶ leadership presence;
▶ key skills and roles for leading change effectively.

The twenty-first century has brought with it many complex challenges for the early years sector in different parts of the world, with a global agenda of reform signifying that it has become increasingly politicized (Baldock et al. 2013). Today, those working in early years provision have a professional responsibility to keep informed about and appropriately responsive to the increasing diversity, complexity and volatility of modern society (Anning et al. 2009). Given the range of factors and forces that impact on contemporary society and consequently on the early years sector, everybody who is associated with early years provision, including leaders, practitioners, families, associated professionals and related bodies, benefits from the development of positive attitudes to and advanced skills for meeting new challenges. We live in a rapidly changing world and the pace, scope and degree with which change continues to occur demand significant adjustment from members of the early years sector.

Not every early years practitioner willingly embraces demand, need and opportunities for reform and change. Despite this, continuing financial constraints and accountability, limitations with human resources and complex professional responsibilities necessitate different ways of working with and for young children and families. Some early years professionals report that they feel uncomfortable with the rapidity and level of proposed changes, giving rise to some degree of confusion, anxiety and stress. However, it is not change itself that is the issue here. Generally, it is individual perceptions about how we personally will be affected, how we will cope and how much control we will have over what happens to us that determine personal reaction to change.

Today, investment in competent leadership within the early years sector will ensure that quality improvement is achieved through the implementation of professionally responsible government reform (Nutbrown 2012). The following four questions (amended from Sullivan's (2010) conversations with other early years educators) focus attention on several important issues for those aspiring to or responsible for leading change.

- How do early years professionals find effective ways to lead change?
- How do those leading change successfully guide people through the process?
- How do those leading change use vision and relationships to inspire and motivate commitment to change?
- What training and professional development opportunities can leaders offer that help enhance knowledge and skills concerning change?

Competent leadership in early years settings can leverage the process of change (that is, assist and advance implementation of a reform agenda) because it concentrates on the what, why, when, who and how of change for those involved. Authentic leadership in early years provision can promote, influence and facilitate the process of change by providing focus, opportunities for participation and building practitioners' confidence to pursue different ways of working. Authentic leadership provides direction, order and support for those affected by change (Aigner 2011) and it lays the foundation for honest relationships, collaboration, self-direction, creativity, innovation and empowerment.

Authentic leadership supports complicated change when it is grounded in 'people influence', that is, power *with* team members, creative collaboration, critical reflection and continuous learning. Change generally meets with less opposition and resistance when every member in a workplace, including early years settings, is an actively engaged and committed collaborator who participates in and contributes to co-creating the way forward to meet continuing professional challenges.

> I think leading change in early years provision today is more about asking questions, facilitating dialogue and stimulating exchange of communication and ideas between the people involved. It is not always about creating a vision or giving direction but getting people thinking and talking about what is needed in the here and now.
>
> Coordinator, integrated childcare centre

How leadership is defined, how early years practitioners understand it, and how it is exercised is of paramount importance in the current climate of reform and change within the sector. The early years workforce is uniquely characterized by diversity of age, experience and training. Consequently, those leading change within it are perceived as more authentic when they match their leadership and communication styles to the expectations of staff. For example, practitioners from across three generations are usually employed within early years provision, including older 'Baby Boomers', middle-aged 'Generation X' and the younger 'Generation Y'. Positional and formal leadership is not confined to older or more experienced employees and it is common to find younger graduates as leaders of early years provision.

Interestingly, each of the generations tends to hold specific values and beliefs about authentic leadership and participation. Baby Boomers (aged late 50s–60s) value freedom of choice but like leaders to be experts who use knowledge and information to guide followers; Generation X (mid 30s–40s) value their own ideas and experience rather than those of an expert and prefer leaders to come from and lead from within the team; whereas Generation Y (20s–early 30s) have been immersed in the concept and skills of leadership from school age, they are independent, want to input into decision-making and expect leadership to be participatory and distributed (Scherer and Efozie 2013). 'Generation Z' (born since 2000) will soon enter the early years workforce. This cohort is described as advantaged, sophisticated, connected and 'technologically savvy' (Keegan 2011). In the workplace, it is anticipated that they will be more self-directed and less interested in teamwork. Consequently, very young members of staff may experience difficulties in meeting the collaborative expectations of today's early years provision.

> Our director has been here for over 20 years now. She is great but she spends a lot of time out doing other things, talks and research mostly. For us, the deputy is our key person. She spends time on the floor and really understands the daily grind of working with children. The director has worked on the floor but not for a long time now, so I think she's a little out of touch with our concerns about the framework and the changes, especially for the newest staff.
>
> Early years teacher, early learning centre

Those who successfully lead change can usually adapt their approach to meet the profile, beliefs and expectations of team members. However, authentic leaders of early years settings generally adopt a non-authoritarian approach, adhere to honest and open communication, and embrace collaborative lifelong learning and development. These key factors also determine how successfully complex change is effected. Although positional leaders in early years provision may hold responsibility for orchestrating and driving change, it is important to bear in mind that individual practitioners are responsible for implementing and embedding it into each setting's culture and systems. It is essential that those leading change are aware of underlying and subconscious orientations to, and beliefs about, leadership and participation by all concerned with change.

The complex reform expected in early years provision today relies upon authentic leadership that is matched to the needs of contexts and practitioners. The specific focus of this chapter is an examination of the type of leadership practice that, regardless of position, qualifications and experience, is more likely to result in the successful implementation of proposed changes within early years provision. A fuller discussion of leadership with reference to aspects of change in early years contexts can be found in other literature including Aubrey (2011), McDowall Clark and Murray (2012) and Rodd (2013a).

Quality improvement through competent leadership

Those who aspire to and are willing to enact leadership play a critical role in ensuring that current government directives and professional expectations for change in the early years are instigated, addressed and successfully achieved. Research evidence in many countries has shown that competent leadership consistently is associated with quality early years provision as well as innovative, responsive change within the sector (Moyles 2006; Dunlop 2008; Garvey and Lancaster 2010; Sharp et al. 2012).

Delivering high quality early years provision in uncertain and financially austere times has become a critical challenge for today's leaders. Competent leadership is the driving force behind improving quality (Reed and Canning 2012), raising standards and achievements (Lindon 2010), enhancing professionalism (Moyles 2006) and increasing accountability (Mathers et al. 2012). Recently in England, the Chief Inspector of the Office for Standards in Education (Ofsted), Sir Michael Wilshaw, commented that incompetent and unstable leadership was linked to children's provision judged to be failing by Ofsted standards (Puffett 2013). In addition, he observed that a high turnover of senior practitioners and directors (32 per cent in 2013 compared with 19 per cent in 2008/9) was detrimental to improving early years provision and recommended that ineffective and incompetent leadership be addressed immediately.

It is evident that targets for quality improvement in early years provision cannot be achieved without recognizing the importance of and developing leadership potential, competence, authenticity and capacity. Change and leadership are inextricably interwoven (Dunlop 2008; Sharp et al. 2012). Change without capable leadership can result in confusion, distrust, disunity, disturbance and sometimes rebellion. In early years provision, where demand for increasingly complex change is ongoing, authentic leadership shows the way and raises the bar in the pursuit of advancement and excellence.

Very simply, leadership in the early years refers to a set of processes that are employed intentionally in order to influence practitioners and relevant others to commit to and work to achieve shared goals. It is primarily a people-oriented process, role and responsibility and evolves out of a leader's personal ability to inspire, encourage, enable, guide, support and empower practitioners to fulfil their potential in a workplace culture that values commitment, challenge, learning and growth. Authentic leadership is recognized from the honest, trusting, meaningful and values-driven relationships developed with colleagues. Those who are accepted as authentic and competent leaders in early years settings endorse the following tenets through their values and action.

- *Every early years practitioner, regardless of position, qualifications and experience has the right and responsibility to engage in leadership.*

The traditional view of leadership being invested in one role and enacted by one person, termed 'positional leadership', has been replaced by a more contemporary viewpoint where competent leadership is considered to be a distributed function and responsibility within and across a range of practitioners and teams. Personal choice is a distinctive attribute of contemporary leadership because it is an individual who chooses, for whatever reasons, to accept and commit to its roles and responsibilities. Leadership, at its very basic, is about making yourself useful and using your time purposively (Aigner 2011), therefore it can be displayed in many forms at any level of experience and responsibility. Individuals who choose to embrace leadership roles and responsibilities can be identified in every position within early years settings. Today, leadership is not necessarily restricted to those holding formal positions of authority. While the context in which leadership is enacted is influential (Hujala 2013), it is the individual leader who chooses the way in which leadership is embraced, personified and exercised (Rodd 2013a).

How individuals choose to enact the process of leadership is critical to whether or not followers endorse them as authentic leaders. Indeed, increasing the number of suitable practitioners who aspire to and consciously choose to develop their personal capacity for leadership has become a pressing concern in contemporary early years provision (Urban et al. 2011; Puffett 2013).

Effective leaders possess insight and ability to perceive both the explicit and obvious and the implicit and underlying demands and needs of a situation requiring leadership, and match or adapt their leadership style in ways that engage and empower others to respond and contribute to positive and improved outcomes for young children and families, early years professionals and provision, and the sector as a whole.

Although experienced and acknowledged leaders of early years provision appreciate that leadership incorporates different facets and functions, for example expert, facilitator, teacher, encourager, supporter, rescuer,

empowerer, helper and learner, some report that they find it difficult to identify, unpick, articulate and illuminate its complexities in practical enactment
(Aubrey et al. 2013). Leadership does not lie in a checklist of qualities and
skills. Competent leadership in early years settings is holistic, dynamic and
creates its own synergy, where interaction between the varying elements
(for example, context, leader and practitioners) produces a greater result
than would the sum of the individual parts. These factors also contribute to
the challenge of defining, researching and enacting leadership in the early
years.

- *Effective leadership comes about via a collective professional philosophy that values and celebrates shared, collaborative participation for
  achieving a vision and a workplace culture that allows and ensures
  that leadership is genuinely diffused and distributed through all levels
  within a setting.*

As early years contexts become increasingly diverse (Edwards 2009; Sharp
et al. 2012), the concept of distributed leadership is regarded as advanta-
geous for meeting growing and disparate challenges. However, it is not simply delegated or handed down. Rather, to be genuinely distributed, leadership needs to be subtly infused throughout workplace values and culture,
and pervade every aspect of an early years setting's operational functioning. Distributed leadership is understated and nuanced, not calculated or
improvised.

According to Waniganayake (2013: 72), ' . . . leadership understandings
emerge through diverse experiences and employment roles'. Aubrey et al.
(2013) suggest that early years professionals hold different ideas about
leadership roles (that is, guide, strategist, motivator, business-oriented)
according to their qualifications. Consequently, it is important that early
years professionals are encouraged to have access to and find opportunities
to enact leadership within their day-to-day work. In a climate of reform and
change for early years provision, leadership can be effective only when it is
properly distributed. Rodd (2013a: 16) defines distributed leadership as ' . . .
the product of the collective endeavor of an interconnected group of early
childhood practitioners where:

- shared, collaborative and collective leadership is evidenced;
- diversity is viewed as a strength for responding to constantly changing
  demands;
- authentic and credible authority is conferred on those who are perceived
  as professional, possessing high levels of expertise, judgement, fairness
  and wisdom; and
- power, defined as influence and strength, is derived from working
  collaboratively with others'.

Leadership in early years settings is a subtle phenomenon that is embedded in social relationships and experience, service structure and context. Its enactment can be difficult, even impossible, to pinpoint and observe. In some situations, effective leadership is displayed through action while in other situations it is enacted by standing back, saying or doing nothing.

> I've heard leadership described as walking backwards with your arms open, it's about communicating direction and encouragement and making space and opening gaps for staff to step up.
>
> Manager, childcare centre

Authentic leaders are able to recognize when it is appropriate to step back, create, open up and broaden spaces that allow others to assume leadership roles and exercise leadership responsibility (Altvater et al. 2005; Ord et al. 2013).

- *Encouraging every early years professional to understand that, by personally taking up leadership roles and responsibilities, they contribute to a pool of potential and budding leaders.*

Evidence suggests that leadership continues to remain an enigma for many; it is not a concept that is clearly defined and confidently grasped within and across the global early years sector (Rodd 2013a). If the early years workforce remains unclear about what leadership entails in the diversity of settings, too few will aspire to, identify with and choose to take up leadership functions. A deficiency of authentic and capable leaders leaves the early years sector in a vulnerable position, particularly when pressure for reform and improvement makes even greater demands for competent and resourceful leadership.

At present, there is no commonly accepted and prevailing definition of leadership in the early years sector. Given the sector's complexity and evolving nature, and the diversity of factors that impact upon it, perhaps the pursuit of a finite definition of leadership has become redundant. Informed understanding about what makes an effective early years leader is more likely to grow out of the organic processes of thinking, sharing and reflection rather than from activity focused on the production of a convergent and potentially static definition.

- *Authentic leadership in early years provision is values-based and values-driven, focused upon improving the future and well-being of all concerned.*

Genuine leadership in early years settings is essentially underpinned by and embedded in values (both personal and professional), knowledge, understanding, relationships, experience and context. It is multi-dimensional, multi-layered, complex and yet holistic in practice. It is conducted in challenging contexts, where staff, families and local communities may have complex and varying needs and expectations, and where pressure for change is endemic.

In addition, leadership is a phenomenon that is greatly influenced by cultural and country-specific characteristics, factors and issues (Rodd 2013b). Leadership styles that are modelled on western values may not be acceptable to or understood by practitioners (or indeed children and families) of different heritages. Not all cultures and countries share the same assumptions about the values, motivations and practice that have styled effective leadership in contemporary western societies such as those in Britain, Australia, New Zealand, Scandinavia, North America and western Europe. Because pressure for change often elicits strong emotional reactions that are linked to personal values, attitudes, politics and experiences, cultural and country-specific factors are likely to affect stakeholders' position on change. This is an important consideration in early years provision where diversity in staff and families can produce unanticipated expectations, approaches and reactions to demands for and leadership of change.

Knowledge about and understanding of one's personal and professional values help human beings make personal connections with and find meaning in even the most mundane aspects of life and work. Because most early years professionals endorse and adhere to a strong professional value system that generally is congruent with their personal values, they tend to perceive their work more as a vocational choice focused on commitment to assisting others, rather than a pathway to personal and financial advantage. Consequently, they are more likely to commit to change proposals that they believe will contribute to improving others' well-being.

In essence, authentic leadership for effecting change in early years settings requires personal capability for:

- inspiring vision and motivating commitment to shared goals;
- engendering trust and respect through the personification of values and beliefs, and principled action;
- transparent communication and quality interpersonal relationships;
- understanding, investing in and developing stakeholders' potential;

as well as a set of 'hard skills' such as flexible thinking, forward planning, decision-making, problem-solving, ability to put plans into action and goal achievement.

Despite the complexity and range of factors that impinge on leadership, it can be useful for even experienced leaders to deconstruct leadership into its component parts. Authentic leaders continually engage in self-reflection about how they personify and enact leadership, especially when confronted with pressure to lead teams through changing times.

While various models and frameworks incorporate different elements to construct a comprehensive picture of what underpins effective leadership, the following sections highlight the contribution of important attributes, skills and roles to understanding what makes an authentic leader during times of change. However, keep in mind that genuine leadership grows out of fully integrated qualities, skills and roles, as well as professional knowledge, understanding, judgement and maturity. It does not emerge from a bundle of indiscriminate component parts. Capable, authentic and effective leadership in early years provision is purposeful, holistic and creates synergy.

The power of leadership presence

Regardless of context, authentic leaders, including those in early years provision, consistently display a set of personal attributes that are recognized and valued by colleagues as contributing to genuine and respected leadership. Given that demand for change can produce distrust, confusion and disruption, the calibre of leadership is pivotal to the early years sector's capacity to meet the current challenges.

'Leadership presence' is a more recent concept in contemporary discussion about who becomes (that is, the type of practitioner) and is endorsed as an authentic leader in early years provision. This concept relates to a debate about the difference between and impact of leaders who are called 'charismatic' and those who are described as 'having presence'. While both concepts incorporate notions of energy, enthusiasm and interpersonal competence, fundamental differences in orientation and outcome are perceived and experienced by others.

In the early years sector, the term 'presence' when applied to leadership paints a professional who is perceived by others as confident, grounded, values-driven, other-oriented, humble, shunning unwarranted attention, gracious, calm, composed under pressure, understated and focused on the betterment of all concerned – in other words, authentic. Colleagues are more likely to trust, respect and follow leaders who transmit a sense of presence (Su and Wilkins 2013).

On the other hand, 'charisma' appears to be derived from perceptions about extroverted personal magnetism and appeal, or a kind of charm and attractiveness that others find interesting and fascinating (Yukl 1999). Charismatic leaders are often depicted as focused on themselves and oriented more towards enhancing their own goals and ambitions. Politicians tend to be described as 'having a certain charisma' whereas world leaders such as Mother Teresa, Mahatma Gandhi and Nelson Mandela are recognized more as 'having a strong presence'. In relation to leadership in early years provision, Dunlop (2012: xii) comments that her ' . . . thinking about leadership has moved beyond the charismatic'.

Su and Wilkins (2013) define leadership presence as the ability to consistently and clearly communicate personal and professional values while engaging, connecting with and influencing others. In early years settings, authentic leadership is communicated through presence and appears to encourage authenticity in others (Leeson 2010). Early years leaders who transmit a sense of presence tend to be regarded by colleagues as having and displaying considerable integrity and dignity, as well as being insightful, confident, energetic and capable. They appear to be more interested in others than themselves, trustworthy and trusted, givers rather than takers, and strong yet vulnerable, and encourage such qualities in others.

Much has been written about the specific attributes that are associated with effective early years leadership and numerous features have been identified (Moyles 2006). Evidence collected in various countries and occupations (Kouzes and Posner 2012) specifically signposts *honesty* (the foundation of trust), *forward-looking* (an orientation to the future), *inspiration* (the power to engage others) and *competence* (the power to act and deliver) as four critical attributes displayed by authentic leaders. Most early years professionals agree that these four characteristics are fundamental to competent leadership (Rodd 2013a). They are also similar to traits associated with 'presence' and are important attributes for those who wish to lead change.

Other important attributes have been identified in theory, research and practice as vital for authentic leadership and consequently presence. The following list is not inclusive but illustrates the type and range of personal attributes that generally underpin leadership presence:

- integrity, exemplary character and trustworthiness;
- courage and confidence;
- openness and honesty;
- ethical and moral in words and action;
- dedication, persistence and commitment;
- energy, enthusiasm and optimism;
- assertive, decisive, yet tolerant of ambiguity;
- emotional intelligence and resilience;
- responsible;
- sense of humour.

In addition, self-awareness and self-knowledge, self-respect and respect for others, investment in the empowerment of others, behaviour grounded in and aligned with values and vision are other features that have been associated with authentic leadership presence in a range of fields, including the early years.

Leadership presence appears to grow out of knowing and feeling comfortable about who you are as a person and as a professional, behaving consistently with your values and beliefs and acting to improve the well-being of others.

> For me as a leader it is all about respect, the workplace atmosphere, the culture, the staff attitudes, our practice, it's all based on mutual respect. If we lost that, we would not be able to offer a quality service for children and families, let alone make significant changes.
>
> Manager, childcare centre

Leadership presence is a powerful force that helps practitioners to identify who they think is authentic and capable of effecting change in early years settings. Those who possess presence are judged as having 'something special' and a certain gravitas that practitioners pick up from subtleties in character, style and substance. Because leadership is the driving force behind sustainable change in early years provision, it is essential that those who aspire to or enact leadership responsibilities possess, acquire and strengthen those attributes that communicate substantial leadership presence to others during the diverse and unpredictable situations that complex change can bring.

Leadership skills for making change happen

While leadership presence is important, competent leadership is associated with a particular set of skills (Rodd 2013a). Those who are responsible for effecting change in early years provision need to identify, develop and sharpen the relevant skills and competencies that underpin leadership practice. According to Harris and Spillane (2008: 33), ' . . . it is the nature and quality of leadership practice that matters'.

Given that responding to change is a critical leadership role and responsibility, those who aspire to and hold responsibility for leading change in early years provision need to be competent in a range of diverse yet essential skills. While the essential contribution of higher-order thinking, conceptual and analytical skills (for example, decision-making, problem-solving) cannot be underestimated, the following abilities reflect the value of the human side of leading change and highlight the power of people in effecting change:

- interpersonal competence, that is, the ability to connect with, inspire and engage others through empathy, vision, communication and emotional intelligence;
- ability to work with a wide range of people, regardless of age, position, qualifications, experience and background;
- investment in lifelong learning;
- willingness and ability to distribute leadership through all levels;
- ability to build collaborative teams;

- confidence and capability to address conflict;
- supervisory, mentoring and coaching skills.

These abilities help those who wish to or are responsible for leading change in early years settings to:

- clearly articulate why change is necessary;
- appreciate the impact of proposed change on work and colleagues;
- change themselves first and so become a role model for change;
- 'walk the talk', show change in behaviour and action rather than telling people how to change;
- realistically assess risk;
- 'sell' change to colleagues and senior administrators;
- monitor and report on progress;
- maintain focus on the vision in a changing context;
- convey credibility to a wide range of people;
- stick with the process despite obstacles and setbacks;
- appreciate their limitations and seek assistance if necessary.

Becoming an effective leader of change is not an easy task. Unfortunately, the presentation of lists of qualities, skills and roles, such as the above, can be daunting, overwhelming and disheartening. And it is true that it takes time and effort to develop attributes that encourage and enable those leading change in early years settings to confidently and competently rise to the challenge. However, many early years practitioners know that they are equal to the task because they hold a fundamental belief about and confidence in their ability to learn. Many early years professionals agree with John Fitzgerald Kennedy's comment that 'Leadership and learning are indispensable to each other', and think that many of the qualities and competencies required to perform leadership roles and responsibilities can be learned and acquired.

Today, the majority of early years professionals accept, as part of their professional identity and responsibility, an ethical obligation to improve the quality of early years experience and provision. This obligation underpins the motivation for continuous learning, improvement and refinement of personal qualities and capabilities as well as professional knowledge, abilities and expertise.

Our coordinator put it like this: change can involve risks but we will only make progress if we think of ourselves as pioneers, learners and explorers, not as cautious followers who do what they are told to do.

Early years educator, pre-school centre

The early years profession's desire to learn scaffolds and supports the acquisition of requisite qualities and skills for the level of leadership competence required to effect proposed changes.

Leadership roles for addressing change initiatives

Put simply, a leader generally is perceived as someone who communicates a vision in order to influence others to commit to and follow that direction.

> *Leadership is the capacity to translate vision into reality.*
> Warren Bennis

In order to leverage progress towards agreed goals, those who aspire to or take up leadership have to fulfil certain roles. Roles describe what leaders do, the core competencies required in leadership activity; they are different from the personal attributes and skills associated with authentic leadership. Although making change happen is not the sole responsibility of any one person (it relies on the commitment and contribution of everyone concerned), change will not happen if those leading it do not successfully undertake specific roles. The deconstruction of leadership roles for change can define and clarify them, and help pinpoint functions that may require attention and improvement. The more informed and prepared early years practitioners are to undertake specific roles, the more effective they will be in leveraging change.

There are a number of classifications that describe the various roles and functions that those leading change perform, with the most basic and general leadership roles including:

- establishing the need and reasons for change;
- determining common goals;
- being a visible, influential and supportive guide through the implementation process.

To be successful in these basic roles, those who lead change, be it simple or more complicated, have to act as the primary advocate and voice for change, become a consistent, positive role model, continue to motivate everyone who is involved, make confident decisions and ensure that change is effected though everyone's participation and contribution (Stagl 2011).

> For me, leading change is about making hard decisions and making sure that everyone involved commits to implementing them. I know it sometimes makes me unpopular with the team but I see it as one of my important responsibilities.
> Director, pre-school centre

However, effecting complicated change requires a type of leadership that compels others to connect, engage and contribute. Recently, Siraj-Blatchford and Hallet (2013) coined the term 'caring leadership', referring to a type of leadership that focuses on sharing and distribution of responsibilities. Because leadership in early years provision can be a complex and elusive concept, it may be useful to define its pertinent roles more specifically. Those leading change should be able to competently fulfil the following roles:

- determining common values and creating a shared vision;
- inspiring, energizing and empowering those concerned;
- communicating in transparent, honest and accessible ways;
- facilitating cooperation and contribution through leading by example and fostering collaborative efforts;
- promoting collective responsibility and teamwork, delegating decision-making and problem-solving in empathic and respectful ways;
- opening space for distributed and collective leadership;
- mentoring practitioners and teams to motivate learning, development and contribution;
- developing strategic plans, goals and procedures cooperatively;
- monitoring progress without micromanaging team members' efforts.

Such lists can be intimidating for aspiring and experienced leaders of early years provision but it is important to appreciate the breadth and depth of competence required to lead complex change. Fortunately, it is rare that those who aspire to or hold responsibility for leadership need to employ all of the skills simultaneously. It is more common for insightful leaders to identify a particular skill or set of skills that would be relevant for specific situations and issues, and ensure that several practitioners possess or acquire ability in the requisite skills.

> I try to be as honest as I can be with the staff and families about what we are facing with these changes. If they don't trust me to tell them about the hard parts as well as the benefits, I'll lose their respect. I don't fudge just how challenging making some of the necessary changes will be, I just remain calm and optimistic that we can do it.
>
> Manager, childcare centre

Appelbaum and Paese (2003) propose an alternative classification of leadership roles for effecting change. This framework focuses on strategic leadership of change (which is completely different from change management). These authors argue that to effect change various strategic functions must be assumed by team members, not necessarily by the positional leader. The important issue for leading change is that the following roles are competently filled by at least one team member.

- **Navigator** – analyses complex issues, problems and situations to identify cause and effect, opportunities and threats, levers and options for overcoming obstacles.
- **Strategist** – develops a long-term plan that is aligned with vision and values.
- **Entrepreneur** – identifies, assesses risks and takes advantage of opportunities for improvement.
- **Mobilizer** – builds a network of collaborative relationships and teams that are empowered to achieve goals and objectives.
- **Talent advocate** – identifies and selects the right people with the right skills for the right task, mentors the development of a broad skills base.
- **Captivator** – inspires others' passion for, commitment to and ownership of the vision and action plan.
- **Global thinker** – a 'leading learner' who motivates others' learning, thinking and development, promotes a culture of learning and integrates information from diverse perspectives.
- **Change driver** – embraces change, works to create new mindsets and challenges the system and status quo with goals of improvement.
- **Enterprise guardian** – defends courageous or unpopular yet appropriate decisions, ensures that progress towards goals continues to be aligned with the vision and ensures that achievement is valued and recognized.

Such functions provide direction for those leading change to transition from a routine management perspective to one of strategic leadership for the complicated, diverse and challenging problems faced in today's early years settings. Those leading change are not expected to be solely responsible for all of these functions, but through a culture of distributed leadership must create opportunities for practitioners to assume some of them. Authentic leaders will be aware of which specific roles and functions match appropriately to practitioners.

> The changes that our service needs to make have forced me to look closely at what each individual team member is capable of contributing. I am looking for people to do certain things, take on specific tasks and be useful in certain situations. Until we had to face up to such big changes, I hadn't fully appreciated some of the team's subtle qualities and competencies. But now that I can see their individual differences and strengths I can start to encourage them more appropriately.
>
> Team leader, early learning centre

Broadly, the roles that those leading change in early years provision undertake include:

- gaining overall commitment to vision, values, policies and plans;
- aligning and integrating practitioners' personal goals with those of the setting and sector;
- canvassing and generating support and cooperation from stakeholders;
- interpreting and executing action plans;
- easing transitions through the processes and stages of change with encouragement, guidance, empowerment and mentoring;
- representing and advocating on behalf of stakeholders, settings and the sector.

While deconstructing some of the attributes, skills and roles associated with competent leadership of change can be helpful, it is important to remember that leadership is purposeful, holistic and synergetic. Competent leadership is more than a display of and proficiency in particular attributes, abilities and roles. It arises out of the interaction among certain combinations of qualities, skills and roles that are matched to meet the demands of specific contexts and available expertise. It is the degree of congruity between all of the crucial elements that determines whether change will be competently led.

> If I were honest, I'd have to say none of us, the team working with children, really likes change. I know other centres are up for it and see it as exciting but as for us, I don't think we're ready for it. We have some new and less experienced practitioners who are still learning the ropes and lack confidence about coping with more pressure. Some of our untrained staff are very negative about being assessed too. It's will be a big job for the coordinator to get everyone to be positive about what she says needs to be done.
>
> Early years team leader, childcare centre

In summary, effecting change through competent authentic leadership entails:

- accepting the need, pressure and demands for change;
- initiating momentum by visibly embracing and defining the what and why of change;
- communicating an explicit vision for improvement;
- leading practitioners and teams in co-created strategic action plans;
- championing change by regularly evaluating the status quo against a vision for change.

Those leading the proposed changes currently demanded in early years provision must develop the ability to anticipate, envision and empower others to work together collaboratively to meet professional responsibility and political demands for improvement. It is their responsibility to initiate, energize and drive identified change while taking steps to overcome or eliminate obstacles and barriers to implementation. A transformational style of leadership is considered most effective for addressing the current change agenda, particularly because ethical dimensions will need to be considered. A transformational leadership style helps leaders to explain the need for change, use leadership presence to create and inspire commitment to the vision and values that guide change, and ensure that change is effected through ongoing commitment and collaboration of stakeholders.

Closing thoughts

In the current political and professional climate, those leading change in early years provision have a lot to do; they have a wide range of responsibilities for and with a diverse range of people. Competent and authentic change leaders at every level within the sector are proactive, inspire through vision, are clear communicators and listeners, value their colleagues, are risk-takers and resourceful, and are committed to lifelong learning. They possess drive, intuition, empathy and a strong moral compass. Leading change in early years settings is a challenging endeavour because it is undertaken in addition to and at the same time as other routine work. This generation of early years practitioners must be committed to embracing change as a means of pursuing and achieving the highest possible quality of provision. With this in mind, those leading change need the full commitment and contribution of others to realize a vision for quality improvement.

3

LEADERSHIP: THE FUEL DRIVING QUALITY IMPROVEMENT

> *Managers are people who do things right,*
> *while leaders are people who do the right thing.*
> Warren Bennis

This chapter explores:

▶ why leadership underpins and drives quality improvement;
▶ how leadership differs from management;
▶ the contribution of leadership to effecting change;
▶ the impact of complexity on leading change;
▶ a model for leading the process of complex change.

Currently, the early years sector in many countries is under pressure to respond to government directives for major reform around goals of quality improvement in provision. Unfortunately, government departments have been slow to publicly acknowledge the essential contribution of leadership to raising standards and improving quality in early years provision. However, the role of competent leadership is now regarded (by both government departments and the sector) as critical for determining how smoothly and effectively early years professionals are able to respond to change directives and targeted outcomes.

The relationship between leadership and quality

Competent leadership in early years settings fans the flame of vision, passion and enthusiasm, stokes the fire of energy that drives action and sustains movement towards enhanced quality in early years provision. Without leadership, early years settings may appear to function satisfactorily on a day-to-day basis. However, practitioners are unlikely to be sufficiently inspired and motivated to put in the sustained work required to achieve the types of professional outcomes that are currently expected and will be expected in the future.

The process of initiating, implementing, coordinating and sustaining change is described by a range of terminology that includes managing, dealing with, adapting to, coping with, responding to and leading change. However, two terms have dominated the literature and therefore modern ideas about change – one is 'management' and the other is 'leadership'. One of the critical issues when exploring the process of change, especially related to quality improvement, is whether it is a function of management or whether it is a leadership responsibility. That is, for change to be successfully implemented and sustained, is it managed or led? Or indeed does it require input from both sets of functions?

Much of the early years literature suggests that efficient operation of settings requires both collaborative management and distributed leadership (Urban et al. 2011). However, too many early years practitioners continue to accept management as the dominant approach for achieving operational effectiveness, including making change happen, within early years provision. When it comes to understanding change, the terminology used by early years practitioners is dominated disproportionally by references to 'the management' of change. It seems that many early years professionals persist in using the terms 'management' and 'leadership' as if they are synonymous and interchangeable when applied to the intricate process of effecting change (Rodd 2013a).

To compound the issue, many of those in formal positions of authority in non school-based early years provision are referred to as 'managers'. However, it is essential for every early years practitioner to understand that leadership is quite different from management, and that managers, capable though they might be, are not necessarily leaders and do not necessarily possess the critical abilities needed to drive change forward. Although leaders in many workplaces, including early years settings, are often expected to undertake some management functions as part of their overall role and responsibilities, the specific orientation of leadership (towards organizational viability, improvement and sustainability) is, by definition, quite different from that of management.

It is true that the successful initiation, implementation and sustainability of complex change in organizations, including early years provision, requires that both leadership and management functions are successfully undertaken (Lindon and Lindon 2012). However, management perspectives are too narrowly focused to effect complex change, and it is leadership that offers an effective combination of attributes, understandings and capabilities to drive change forward (Kouzes and Posner 2012). Nevertheless, to successfully implement and secure change in early years provision, the two approaches must operate efficiently and appropriately to achieve specific goals. Early years settings operate effectively only when they are both competently managed and expertly led. This is even more important when demand for quality improvement through complicated reform proposals is experienced. Because those leading change should not be overburdened by management tasks, and given the different orientations of leadership and management, rarely will one person be able to competently fulfil these different lines of action simultaneously.

> Even the terms used to describe our position show confusion about leadership and management. Some of us are called directors, some are called coordinators and some of us are called managers, . . . and we all do pretty much the same job. The only time leadership is mentioned is if you are called team leader, but that is leading a team, not being the leader of a setting.
>
> Coordinator, childcare centre

Differentiating leadership from management

Management is the term that was used to explain the process of establishing order and consistency in the large work organizations that emerged during the twentieth century. As a skill set, management focuses on keeping organizations on track, on time and on budget. It is concerned with planning and balancing income and expenditure, and the allocation of resources to achieve short-, medium- and long-term targets and measurable goals. It is focused on matching people to tasks, jobs and roles as well as delegating, monitoring, controlling and problem-solving. Although some managers do possess leadership ability, their core orientation is to preserve the status quo and productivity by keeping people, structures and systems working day after day.

The study of leadership has a very long history and can be dated back to Plato in the literature. Given the twenty-first century's increasing social complexity and demand for individual and workplace flexibility and adaptability, the study of leadership continues to attract considerable interest from a range of employment sectors.

Leadership, in contrast to management, is not primarily concerned with the maintenance of order and consistency. Rather, leadership has the generation of movement for improvement as it core focus (Kotter 1990). Leadership fuels movement towards quality improvement, change and progress because it provides the energy, power, stimulation and encouragement that propels, drives and sustains people and activity. By identifying, assessing and capitalizing on opportunities, competent leadership becomes the fuel for and the driving force behind the creation of better systems and structures for managers to manage.

Because quality improvement is an outcome of competent change leadership, it is a product of movement and innovation, not of preserving the status quo. It is a leader who creates, directs and coordinates change, not a manager who is more focused on maintaining stasis. The current reform directives for early years provision demand quality improvement through change; consequently, capable leadership that drives change is what is required.

> Our director is the one who talks about the future, she uses words like 'big picture' and 'vision' to let us know, . . . you'd say inspire . . . that she wants us to aim for something different.
>
> Early years educator, early learning centre

In brief, leaders are concerned primarily with vision, inspiration, motivation, commitment, contribution, the future, improvement and progress. Leaders, in contrast with managers, tend to be perceived by colleagues as more proactive, flexible, risk-taking and open to new ideas and better ways of working (Rodd 2013a).

According to Kotter (2011: 6), 'Management's mandate is to minimize risk and to keep the current system operating. Change, by definition, requires creating a new system, which in turn always demands leadership'. Many workplaces, including early years settings, suffer from an imbalance between the need for expert visionary leadership and competent workplace administration. Over-emphasis on management can breed an unwillingness and inability to change. However, leadership without management can give rise to instability through a failure to adequately embed and consequently sustain change. For change to be implemented successfully, a balance between the two functions must be achieved. Unfortunately, many early years professionals think that, despite government and professional pressures for reform and improvement, today's provision continues to be over-managed and under-led (Siraj-Blatchford and Hallet 2013); that is, there is too great a focus on preserving *what is* instead of imagining *what could be*.

In the past, some early years leaders tackled complicated structural and systemic change by tinkering around the edge, and fine-tuning current circumstances through minor adjustments or alterations. However, the current change directives for early years provision demand major reorientation to a new reality, require significant adaptation of existing early years structures and systems, and in some cases necessitate a major overhaul, re-creation and possibly transformation of existing structures and systems.

> I know that the reform agenda means I'll have to delegate more to my deputy and the team, and I'll have to give them more support for the tasks they will have to take on, but without delegating some of my duties, I won't be able to meet the new standards expected of the service.
>
> Manager, children's centre

The demands of change proposals around quality improvement are challenging and complex. They require transformational leadership (that is, visionary, inspirational and values-based guidance) as well as efficient management (that is, planning, organization, coordination). To successfully implement and sustain complex reform, those leading it should not be over-loaded with management obligations. However, they do need to ensure that the day-to-day management and operational functions of early years settings are delegated and fulfilled by suitably qualified and experienced practitioners, and that meaningful leadership roles and responsibilities are available, accessible and embraced by as many practitioners as possible.

The contribution of leadership to effecting change

In order to understand the different orientations and contributions of leadership and management, and consequently their disparate outcomes, the early years workforce must be very clear about what distinguishes leadership and sets it apart from management.

The management of early years provision essentially entails responsibility for day-to-day planning, organization and coordination, for example:

- setting goals for individuals and teams;
- agreeing targets and tasks with practitioners and teams;
- creating professional development plans for individual practitioners;
- conducting monitoring, supervisory and disciplinary meetings;
- undertaking recruitment, induction, appraisal and performance interviews.

In early years provision, management ensures that practitioners satisfactorily complete routine, day-to-day housekeeping tasks essential for the smooth operation of a setting (Ebbeck and Waniganayake 2003). It is a necessary skill set but it is not sufficient to successfully power the levels of energy and activity required to meet current demands for complex reform in early years provision.

Interestingly, both Kotter (1999) and Drucker (2007), pioneer authors on organizational behaviour, put forward the idea that people cannot be managed, they only respond to leadership. Quality improvement through the processes of change is pursued by and effected through people. Only people have the power to make change happen. Therefore, leading change in early years provision must focus on inspiring and motivating practitioners and teams towards improvement by:

- initiating and building a shared vision of a better future;
- generating commitment, cooperation and collaboration;
- looking at broad goals and long-term timeframes;

Table 3.1 Functions that differentiate leaders from managers

Leaders	Managers
Innovate	Administer
Develop	Maintain
Originate	Imitate
Rely on trust	Rely on control
Focus on people	Focus on structures and systems
Take a long-range perspective	Take a short-term view
Focus on the horizon	Look at the bottom line
Challenge the status quo	Accept the status quo
Ask what and why	Ask how and when
Draw out the specific strengths and knowledge of every team member	Organize work to maximize efficiency and productivity

Source: Bennis (2009)

- modelling professional values, attitudes and behaviour;
- taking calculated risks to make a difference;
- initiating and guiding the process of change.

Bennis (2009) proposed that certain functions, summarized in Table 3.1, differentiate those who display leadership and those whose focus is management.

It is clear that leaders and managers have different orientations and priorities, and contribute to the operation of a workplace in different ways and at different levels. Understanding the specific contributions of leadership to quality improvement and the enhancement of early years provision includes identifying current and long-range priorities, connecting with colleagues, focusing on and drawing on the strengths and contributions of practitioners, looking for and entertaining new possibilities, making appropriate and timely decisions, aiming for innovative solutions and progress, and working to a future-oriented agenda and timeframe.

The impact of complexity on leading change for improvement

In order to more fully understand change and how to lead it, it is important for early years leaders to appreciate the impact of complexity on the ease and success with which proposed change can be achieved within settings. Although quality improvement through change has been a permanent feature of early years provision for many decades, the kinds of changes that leaders were required to introduce in the past were not as complex as they have been in more recent times. Indeed, the concept of 'change agent' only started to feature as a significant responsibility of leaders of early years provision within the last decade or so. For example, qualified early years teachers in England were recently recognized as agents of change (Urban et al. 2011). However, the vicissitudes of contemporary political, social and economic circumstances and concerns necessitate that every early years practitioner assumes responsibility, in different ways and at different levels, for acting as a change agent to ensure that all provision remains relevant and sustainable.

In past times, the changes that early years leaders were required to oversee were simpler than those of today because in general:

- parameters were known, comprehensible, familiar and predictable;
- they were more routine and replicable on the basis of past experience;
- cause and effect were easier to identify and understand;
- specific expertise usually was not required;
- existing policies and best practice could be applied appropriately.

For example, the 1990s witnessed significant changes to early years education and childcare in England (Kwon 2002). However, the majority of change initiatives were planned, controlled and supervised by government departments and local authorities. Early years professionals, mainly teachers, had little freedom to influence or lead implementation processes, let alone contribute to the vision for or direction of change. In addition, where change proposals were more complicated, they tended to require the coordination of expertise from specialized professionals who were familiar with early years provision. For example, when it was legislated that children with a range of additional needs were to be included within mainstream rather than in special early years provision (Rodgers and Wilmot 2011), early years practitioners had access to some support from external professionals such as advisers, psychologists, speech therapists and physiotherapists.

In those times, early years professionals, who typically were qualified teachers, managed rather than led the implementation of change. However, today's early years professionals expect to contribute to and influence proposed changes for quality improvement, as well as to access varied opportunities for decision-making about, participation in and leadership of change initiatives.

Today, quality improvement in early years provision is complex rather than simple, with many change proposals meeting Glouberman and Zimmerman's (2002) criteria for complex change described below:

- domains and parameters are intangible or vague;
- many critical elements must be addressed, sometimes simultaneously;

- no patterns are evident or currently predictable;
- each situation is unique;
- previous success with change does not guarantee future success;
- existing expertise can assist but is not sufficient;
- positive workplace relationships are key to successful implementation.

In addition, there are many possible pathways and potential approaches to quality improvement in early years provision, the circumstances of individual settings are always in transition and there is no evident end point for achieving quality. The notion of 'quality' defies definition because, in early years provision, it is always growing and changing. The lack of tangibility, certainty and predictability about what to do, and how best to do it, can create uncertainty, stress, friction and hesitation in early years practitioners.

> I read through the documentation that we were sent about the new framework, but I still don't really understand what it means for the service and my work. It's really stressing me out, . . . the coordinator needs to explain it better . . . so I know what is expected, . . . until that happens, I'm just going to do what I've always done. It's raised the tension levels in our staff meetings.
>
> Early years professional, children's centre

When early years leaders and practitioners appreciate the inherent 'unknowability', uncertainty and unpredictability of quality improvement through change, they can appreciate that its successful implementation depends on capable leadership ability that:

- supports those engaged in implementation to make sense of what is happening;
- communicates the importance of becoming resilient to and tolerant of uncertainty;
- identifies, assesses and responds to emerging opportunities, challenges and problems;
- maintains a positive orientation to the 'big picture' and the future;
- works on an evolving plan for monitoring and evaluating action and progress.

Early years practitioners' willingness to commit to effecting complicated change relies on the creation of supportive relationships within settings, the development of a culture of learning and possibility, and empathic guidance by a trusted colleague. These are clearly functions of leadership.

> My approach to this agenda is that 'we're all in it together', so I tell the team about my difficulties in knowing exactly where we're meant to be going and what we're meant to be doing, I need their support as much as they need mine, I need their ideas as much as they need direction form me.
>
> Coordinator, childcare centre

Leadership in early years provision, as within other workplaces, incorporates a range of dimensions that involve various and specific foci, for example,

- **strategic** – the production of policies and long-range plans, critical decision-making and the implementation of actions that shape and guide a better future;
- **administrative** – dealing with management issues related to efficient day-to-day operation;
- **staffing** – attending to motivation, delegation, conflict resolution;
- **pedagogical** – addressing curriculum and educational issues.

Interestingly, some early years leaders argue that smaller settings require a greater focus on pedagogical leadership, whereas larger settings benefit from a greater focus on strategic leadership. However, regardless of a setting's size, and because local operational structures and systems can be altered at any time, early years leaders at every level should become familiar with and acquire skill in each of the above leadership dimensions.

When early years settings experience pressure for quality improvement, it is often appropriate for those leading change proposals to delegate various management functions in order to free up time to devote to the strategic dimension of leadership. In times of change, leaders should not be overburdened with management responsibility. However, it must be remembered that delegation is not the same as creating space and opportunity for distributed leadership throughout settings. Appropriate delegation, where practitioners act as an agent for the leader, is conducted on the basis of individual expertise and competence. For example, the responsibility for pedagogical leadership may be delegated to a practitioner with acknowledged professional expertise and interest in pedagogy. Similarly, a deputy director may take responsibility for particular staffing and budgeting issues. However, when early years provision is under pressure for reform, those leading proposed changes must retain key functions related to strategic planning, motivation and 'incentivization' of others. Their attention and energy must not be distracted or consumed by management functions that could be handled more appropriately by other early years practitioners.

A model for leading complex change

The key to competent leadership of the current reform directives is the ability to identify, understand, address and incorporate all of the critical elements that impact upon the processes of effecting change. When those leading change in early years settings understand how these elements contribute to, interrelate and impact upon making change happen, they are in a better position to make decisions that facilitate rather than impede the process of change.

The critical factors that contribute to complex and sustainable change can be broken down into seven prerequisite elements (adapted from Knoster et al. 2000) and include vision, consensus, skills, incentives, resources, action plan and evaluation.

If any one of these elements is insufficient, inadequately addressed or missing, the desired change will not be effected and unfortunately a different and potentially undesirable outcome may result. This model, summarized in Table 3.2, offers those leading change a structure for evaluating and supporting the introduction of complicated change in terms of the seven elements.

When initiating change or addressing directives for quality improvement, those leading the change proposals are advised to critically analyse and assess the availability of each of the seven elements in early years practitioners, teams and settings. If any one element is inadequate or missing, progress in implementation will be hampered until those leading change act to procure or restore it.

The first step is to ensure there is a clearly communicated *vision*. This is an absolute necessity for focusing on quality improvement and the starting point for early years leaders who are beginning to plan to introduce change. A vision is an expression of the aspirations and goals that give shape to the future. It must generate inspiration, action and transformation of the status quo. Where a vision is inadequate, poorly communicated or indeed absent, practitioners may feel confused and lack a sense of meaning, purpose and direction. When early years practitioners raise the following questions, those leading change have not adequately articulated the vision.

Why should we be interested in doing that?
What does she want us to do?
What is the aim of all of this?
What are 'the powers that be' thinking?
Here we go again! Another magical mystery tour!
Will this really make any difference?

The process of creating a vision in times of change is just as important as the vision itself. Where a vision for quality improvement is co-constructed and a product of collaboration, early years practitioners are more likely to develop a sense of *consensus*, ownership and consequently commitment to its promotion. Consensus grows out of a climate of support, encouragement, shared understanding and purpose, and collegiality. It results from

Table 3.2 Elements affecting complex change

No vision	Consensus	Skills	Incentives	Resources	Action plan	Evaluation	=	**Confusion**
Vision	**No consensus**	Skills	Incentives	Resources	Action plan	Evaluation	=	**Sabotage**
Vision	Consensus	**Lack of skills**	Incentives	Resources	Action plan	Evaluation	=	**Anxiety**
Vision	Consensus	Skills	**No incentives**	Resources	Action plan	Evaluation	=	**Slow progress**
Vision	Consensus	Skills	Incentives	**No resources**	Action plan	Evaluation	=	**Frustration**
Vision	Consensus	Skills	Incentives	Resources	**No action plan**	Evaluation	=	**False starts**
Vision	Consensus	Skills	Incentives	Resources	Action plan	**No evaluation**	=	**Impact unknown**

and enhances the solidarity of a team. However, if an external body or higher authority has imposed top-down and specific proposals for the future, practitioners may remain unconvinced, and subsequently unwilling to engage with or endorse such changes. Some may actively or passively challenge, oppose, resist or attempt to obstruct external pressure and internal efforts to introduce proposed changes. This is a particularly important issue for family-run settings, multi-disciplinary teams and multi-agency provision where negativity and obstructiveness can impede activity towards change. Early years practitioners who do not hold a consensual vision typically make oppositional, challenging, obstructive and undermining statements about change proposals.

> During a training day for family daycare workers, I could sense an underlying negativity and resistance, so I told them in a pleasant but firm voice that they needed to come on board and start to work with the framework. I emphasized that, given the level of support available, I expected them to start to engage with it . . . The coordinators who were present were very pleased that I took that stand; . . . to push them to come to terms with the fact that we have no choice, we all have to learn new skills and make changes in the way we work.
>
> Manager, children's services

Early years practitioners who either possess or have access to the acquisition of relevant *skills* and expertise for meeting change directives tend to approach the process with confidence and optimism. When those leading change identify the knowledge, competencies and expertise required to approach, undertake or negotiate tasks in new ways, early years practitioners become more willing to try out different strategies and put new plans into action. If practitioners do not possess the necessary knowledge, capability and confidence to meet new challenges, they can become anxious about their ability to cope with and consequently unwilling to risk exploring and implementing new ways of working. Their anxiety can be exacerbated if they do not believe that the training and support offered by those leading change will equip them with the necessary skills. Early years practitioners who are anxious about their readiness to cope with demands for change may make the following comments.

I can't do that.
I don't know if I will be able to . . .
How will I fit into the new structure? What will I do?
Why is it taking so long to get this up and running?
How do we move forward with the framework?

When early years leaders specify clear *incentives* and benefits of working to implement proposed changes, practitioners become more willing to invest energy into making change happen. Early years leaders who are familiar with Maslow's (1970) hierarchy of needs appreciate that they can use practitioners' personal needs, interests and concerns to ensure that progress with the implementation of change is sustained (Rodd 2013a). When early years practitioners do not think that they will benefit personally from a proposed change, they are less likely to commit to and work on embedding new practice into day-to-day routines. As a result, progress with implementing change becomes slow. The 'what's in it for me' factor can be very powerful.

Although early years leaders have little scope to offer extrinsic incentives such as additional pay, they can use intrinsic motivators such as improved self-esteem, sense of achievement, special responsibilities, opportunities to create, collaborate and try out new approaches. When there is an absence of incentive, early years practitioners may make the following comments.

What will we get out of doing this?
Things are fine as they are, I can't see any point in changing how we do our work.
We don't need to change anything yet.
This will just mean extra work for us all.
No way, I'm not paid enough to go to meetings after work!
Don't waste my time, we tried it before and it didn't work.
I just want to do my job and not be bothered with these new-fangled demands.

One of the biggest obstacles to timely implementation of change for early years leaders is access to and availability of adequate *resources*. Resources are assets that contribute to making change happen. They may be physical, intellectual, emotional, human, financial and the availability of time. If early years practitioners do not feel that they have sufficient resources to respond to change directives or are blocked by red tape and bureaucracy, they can feel frustrated, thwarted, discouraged and defeated. High levels of frustration can diminish commitment to and the pace of change. Those leading change need to ensure that adequate resources are available and supplied that enable early years practitioners to respond to change proposals. Where insufficient resources are available, early years practitioners may make the following comments.

They expect everything and give nothing.
How can I be expected to do that in my time allocation?
I haven't got the equipment I need to make that happen.
I haven't got the support of my colleagues.
We haven't enough trained staff to put that into practice.

Early years leaders who have properly addressed the critical elements of vision, consensus, skills, incentives and resources still need to ensure that a 'do-able' *action plan* is developed in advance of implementation by the team. An action plan is constructed by working out the steps required to direct action towards achievement of future goals. Action plans work better if they are co-constructed by those leading change and practitioners so that a fuller and consensual understanding of what needs to be done and how it is best done is gained. If there is no action plan or if it is inadequate, early years practitioners will have little sense of direction and won't know what they should be doing. This may result in slow progress, false starts from frequent alterations to direction and strategies, and practitioners feeling as if they are on a treadmill because they continue doing what they have always done. Alternatively, they may just 'do their own thing' because they have not gained a sense of succeeding in working differently or achieving new goals. Successful leaders of change use the adage (ascribed to both Henry Ford and Mark Twain) below to describe what happens when change directives are addressed without an action plan.

If you always do what you've always done,
you'll always get what you've always got.

Where an action plan is absent or inadequate, early years practitioners may make comments such as:

We're going round in circles.
We're not making any progress with this.
We keep talking but nothing is happening.
Too many people are doing things that we haven't agreed on.

Finally, an action plan is not complete until it has been properly evaluated. *Evaluation* is the structured process of assessing the results, value, success and impact of a plan in meeting its goals. It usually includes reference to monitoring strategies and opportunities to reflect upon lessons learned. Experienced early years leaders appreciate that the implementation of change is underpinned by reasons for it – for example, quality improvement. Change is not implemented for its own sake or on an ad hoc basis. In response to pressures for change, some early years settings engage in a flurry of activity. However, without proper evaluation, no one knows whether such activity produces the intended impact or any impact at all. Activity can come to a standstill, early years practitioners can begin to disengage, lose interest, become bored, passive and disinclined to act. Inertia sets in and motivation deteriorates when practitioners do not have access to information about the progress and impact of change processes. Therefore, it is essential to measure the outcome and impact of any plan to implement change.

When evaluated outcomes or impact are communicated, early years practitioners may make comments such as:

I think the new routine has helped improve the children's engagement.
The new way of recording observations has saved me quite a lot of time.

On the other hand, when there is no access to information about evaluation or impact, they may make comments such as:

I tried the new planning format and I can't see any difference at all.
I don't think the new system has changed much, it's the same old stuff repackaged, we just get more of the same messages in different words.

In conclusion, successful introduction, planning for and implementation of complex change for quality improvement is achieved when those leading change in early years settings ensure that:

- a clear vision statement is co-constructed and endorsed by all concerned;
- team consensus and support for vision and strategic planning is achieved;
- skills, knowledge and expertise to complete the tasks exist;
- incentives to motivate practitioners are identified;
- resources to support the completion of tasks are available;
- an action plan to guide and direct practitioners' efforts is constructed;
- an evaluation format that measures progress, outcomes and impact of action plans and shared goals is developed.

Change will happen only when all of these elements are in place. Early years leaders who display expertise in responding to directives for quality improvement in provision accept and assume responsibility for communicating focus, setting priorities, energizing and motivating practitioners and teams, reinforcing and rewarding individual and team investment and commitment, and counteracting potential stress and burnout in practitioners and teams. They delegate appropriate management functions and foster a culture where leadership opportunities are genuinely distributed and accessible throughout early years settings.

Closing thoughts

Any agenda for reform and change in early years provision rests upon competent leadership. Successful leadership of change directives is underpinned by shared and consensual vision, values, meaning and strategies, influence without direct power, collaborative relationships and approaches, ability to tolerate and respond to unpredictability, a culture of and opportunities for learning, and steady progress forward on the basis of well thought out, sensitively implemented and properly evaluated action plans. Competent early years leaders support both practitioners and teams to engage with complex reforms and changes by building strong professional interpersonal relationships through key interpersonal skills, especially communication. These areas are covered in the following two chapters.

4

INTERPERSONAL RELATIONSHIPS: THE FOUNDATIONS FOR EFFECTING CHANGE

*Trust is the glue of life. It's the most essential ingredient in
effective communication. It's the foundational
principle that holds all relationships.*
Steven Covey (2004)

This chapter explores:

▶   the role of interpersonal relationships in change;
▶   the role of trust in developing professional relationships;
▶   the difference between professional relationships and friendships;
▶   key interpersonal skills for leading complex change.

When leading change in early years provision, it is important to appreciate that people are each setting's social capital; it is early years practitioners who provide the resources that underpin the capacity to create, expand, adapt, innovate and change. Today, it is widely acknowledged that leadership is grounded in relationships and is a social and collective process (McDowall Clark and Murray 2012; Nutbrown 2012; Rodd 2013a; Siraj-Blatchford and Hallet 2013). The ease with which change, especially complicated change, is effected in early years provision rests upon the quality of interpersonal relationships between colleagues, administration and leadership. Leadership relies upon and evolves from quality interpersonal relationships in the workplace. Therefore, when early years leaders and practitioners address the complexities of proposed change, it is essential that they first focus on forming and nurturing supportive interpersonal relationships between leaders and practitioners, and among practitioners.

The reality of modern life is that many people spend more time in the workplace with their colleagues than they do at home with family and friends. No workplace can be successful without good interpersonal relationships. In fact, quality interpersonal relationships are the foundation upon which complex workplace activity, such as addressing need and proposals for change, is built. Competent, purposeful leadership helps encourage stability in workplace climate and relationships during the process of change. Insightful leaders in early years settings devote attention and time to building quality interpersonal relationships through the use of key interpersonal skills, especially interpersonal communication. Quality early years provision cannot be achieved without practitioners who are competent in interpersonal relationships, skills and communication (Sims 2011; Hallet 2012). These are also foundation and essential competencies for leading complex change.

Generally, interpersonal relationships are defined as associations or bonds between two or more individuals who share and are committed to common interests, goals and objectives (Johnson 2013). In early years provision, high quality interpersonal connections are evidenced by mutuality, positive regard, vitality and resilience. Such relationships develop out of honesty and transparency, trust and respect, and consideration of and acceptance of others' opinions, ideas and views. Informed leaders of change in early years provision appreciate the importance of the development of positive and constructive interpersonal relationships between colleagues at all levels because such relationships help foster a positive workplace climate, greater mutual understanding, better teamwork, reduced levels of stress and conflict, improved goal achievement and increased productivity (Johnson 2013). Consequently, early years practitioners experience better morale and display greater willingness to engage with the various challenges demanded of those working in the sector.

> If I had to use one word to describe the key to our team, it would be . . . relationships. It's all about relationships with us . . . trust, respect, encouragement . . . these are the most important factors in the way we work together.
>
> Early years teacher, nursery school

Importantly, positive interpersonal relationships in the workplace foster a climate of trust that in turn generates an increased sense of belonging and efficacy (Hood 2012), enhanced commitment, stronger engagement with professional development and learning, mutual support through times of uncertainty, crisis and change, and consequently strong early years communities and networks.

The role of trust in developing professional relationships

In any workplace, leaders play a central role in determining the level of trust and respect among colleagues. Because interpersonal relationships at work can be convoluted, those who lead change effectively in early years settings appreciate the importance of creating genuine bonds and connections between practitioners at all levels by generating the development of trust and loyalty. In times of demanding change, it is especially important that everyone, both leaders and practitioners, experiences a sense of psychological safety. Psychological safety facilitates interpersonal relationships (Eggers 2011) and is built through demonstrated respect, kindness, fairness, personal responsibility and reliability – for example, by leaders and practitioners keeping and following through on commitments and not taking advantage of others, particularly those who might be vulnerable. Psychological safety in early years settings grows out of a willingness to trust other people. Trust itself is generated from consistent and predictable experiences with them.

> Our team totally trusts the director. He is always honest and upfront about any-thing new that affects us, he doesn't 'sugarcoat' the information but conveys real confidence that we're up to meeting the challenge. He would never ask the team to put in place anything that would not be in the best interests of the chil-dren, families, team or the service.
>
>   Early years educator, childcare centre

Trust, a belief and confidence in the honesty, integrity and reliability of others, is the foundation upon which interpersonal relationships are built. Trust is the central value and feature in all quality interpersonal relationships, and it is particularly relevant for early years settings (Moyles 2006). Trust promotes interdependence between practitioners, encourages teamwork and supports experimentation. When early years practitioners know, understand and care about one another as well as the work they undertake, trust increases and subsequently the motivation to commit and cooperate is enhanced. Trust is fundamental to the successful initiation and implementation of change (Hemp and Stuart 2011). Without trust, individual and team relationships can deteriorate, crumble and fracture. If trust is lacking between early years leaders and practitioners and between practitioners themselves, it becomes difficult if not impossible to instigate and address the changes currently required in the sector.

In addition, because status and authority can be intimidating, those who lead change can easily become isolated from other practitioners (O'Connor 2012). Leaders who appear distant and removed from practitioners' day-to-day experiences may weaken and diminish others' trust in them. Those leaders whose words and actions illustrate their authenticity, personal integrity and dependability earn the trust and respect of early years practitioners. Trust and respect in early years provision emerge from day-to-day interpersonal interactions that are grounded in:

- transparent and honest communication;
- commonality of interests, goals and objectives;

- equality, cooperation and teamwork;
- consistency, reliability and predictability.

When trust is low or has not been nurtured in early years provision, cynicism, doubt, anxiety, self-interest and self-preservation may motivate practitioners' attitudes and behaviours, resulting in low energy, interest and productivity. Leaders who foster trusting and respectful interpersonal relationships in early years settings are accessible, listen to, acknowledge and validate practitioners' concerns, are dependable, and follow through on commitments.

According to Stamopoulos (2011), early years leaders who nurture high levels of trust and build strong relationships with team members inspire a sense of optimism, hope and courage to persist, despite obstacles and setbacks. Leaders can also develop increased confidence and determination when they know they have and can rely on back-up from a trusted team. When addressing complicated change, insightful early years leaders appreciate that trust is a necessary prerequisite for genuine engagement, commitment, creativity and innovation by practitioners. Successful implementation of change in early years provision will occur only where an atmosphere of psychological safety and trust exists.

Professional interpersonal relationships in early years settings

Supportive professional relationships are one of the key features of and a necessary condition for successful implementation of complex change in early years provision. When addressing the various change directives regarding improving early years provision, insightful leaders appreciate the importance of interpersonal relationships that are professional, reciprocal, appropriate and supportive. They understand that certain types of relationships can be unhealthy, destructive and non-professional (Hood 2012) and work to impede the progress of change.

Those leading change in early years settings should be aware that workplace relationships typically are complicated and can be precarious. This is particularly true of relationships that may develop between those in positions of power and those that they lead.

During the last two years, I have experienced a lot of personal strain from trying to meet the new guidelines and expectations. When times are tough, the team seem to have each other, I hear them grumbling to one another about this and that. But I can't do that with them, I'm 'the boss'. There needs to be a distance between us in case I have to take hard decisions. But I sometimes feel lonely and wish I had someone at work who I could confide in and just get some of my frustrations out. But I have to wait until I can share my stuff with other coordinators who understand my position.

Coordinator, childcare centre

While it may be tempting, converting a professional relationship at work to one of a friendship can be fraught with difficulties for both parties, especially where there are differences in status and authority. Workplace relationships are at best awkward to negotiate, particularly in people-oriented environments such as early years settings, where the values of teamwork, cooperation and collaboration override traditional hierarchies based on status, position and power. However, the challenges of delivering quality early years provision in the twenty-first century require that early years practitioners examine the type and quality of existing professional interpersonal relationships and ensure that the traditional workplace culture and values of 'niceness and friendship' in professional relationships (Ebbeck and Waniganayake 2003) are transformed into relationships that are grounded in the contemporary values, expectations, behaviours and standards of early years practitioners.

In early years provision, there is a big difference between being a colleague and being a friend. Professional relationships have a different tone compared to friendships (Hood 2012). In early years settings, 'being friendly' is an expected and constructive pattern of behaviour in the workplace that is displayed by being sociable, agreeable, respectful, managing anger and other strong feelings, taking personal responsibility, acknowledging, apologizing and learning from mistakes. In contrast, being a 'friend' involves a special relationship based on mutual and unconditional caring, trust and communication. Friendship implies a different level of sharing and intimacy. Friends are people who know and accept the 'real you' with all your faults and imperfections, those who you trust to help you when you need it, who forgive you when you've done the wrong thing, let yourself or others down, and those who you choose to spend your free time with.

> I thought we'd become friends because we've been working together with the three-year-olds for a long time now. But when I found out that she'd been putting me down to the other staff and taking the credit for the good things we've done with the curriculum, I couldn't believe it! I felt really let down and betrayed . . . she must have known I'd find out. Nobody keeps their mouth shut here . . . I don't think I can trust anyone in this service.
>
> Childcare worker, early learning centre

> I found out the hard way that your boss never can be a real friend . . . that there are real boundaries between friends and colleagues. I thought we had a special relationship but when she gave me some negative feedback, I was devastated. I'd shared things about my personal life that I would not have told her if I didn't think we were real friends. Now I feel exposed and vulnerable, I constantly wonder if she will use what she knows against me. My position feels untenable now.
>
> Manager, child and family provision

The key difference between appropriate relationships with colleagues and friendships is professional respect. Professional respect is displayed through being courteous, polite and considerate, valuing the rights of others, encouraging and listening to others' ideas, opinions and views, valuing others' contributions, using professional and respectful language in communications with others and accepting personal responsibility for meeting professional expectations and standards. Conflict of interest and ethical concerns can emerge when early years leaders and practitioners do not differentiate between professional relationships and friendships. For example, professionals address each other respectfully and maintain confidentiality but friends may not feel similarly obliged.

> One of my professional interpersonal expectations is the use of appropriate forms of address for children and also for colleagues. I don't accept team members using inappropriate terms such as 'Babe', 'Doll', 'Darl', 'Lovey' or worst yet, 'Dude' when on the floor. And I discourage the use of nicknames because they create barriers and can discriminate between staff. I ask the team to use everyone's first name because that is professionally respectful.
>
> Coordinator, childcare centre

Professional interpersonal relationships evolve from ability to trust, respect and function together and build rewarding collaborative working associations.

> When I induct a new practitioner into the service, I inform them that we are here to work, not to make close friendships. I explain that it is important to be friendly with colleagues but that, because we work so closely together for such long hours, friendships can turn sour and petty jealousies and rivalries can build up. As a team, we do meet outside work every now and then for a meal or to celebrate a special occasion but I don't encourage friendships in the workplace because they tend to create problems with and for the team. You know that old saying, it will all end in tears, that's what happens when professional relationships morph into friendships.
>
> Director, early learning centre

Professional interpersonal relationships are defined by boundaries that are inherent and implicit in working in early years provision. They are characterized by warmth, empathy and approachability but maintain a certain emotional distance. They transcend the concept of friendship because the roles of leader, practitioner and team member entail a set of expected behaviours that would never exist in genuine friendships. Finally, professional relationships often incorporate a power differential, whereas friendship is intrinsically a relationship between equals. During times of change, professional relationships can help support early years practitioners through uncertainty, stress and challenge in ways that do not compromise ongoing and future working associations.

Establishing and maintaining professional interpersonal relationships in early years settings contributes to a sense of psychological safety and increasing trust for all concerned. The boundaries inherent in professional early years relationships serve a number of protective purposes. First, boundaries define and control appropriate levels of emotional involvement while permitting practitioners to be empathic, aware of and sensitive to each other's feelings, developing greater mutual understanding and encouraging appropriate responding. Second, boundaries serve an ethical purpose by helping to maintain clarity of focus, thinking and problem-solving and ensure that decision-making is in the best interests of all concerned. Finally, boundaries support professional emotionally intelligent coping mechanisms that ensure personal needs are met through self-discipline and self-care.

In early years provision, where practitioners do not understand or respect the benefits of professional interpersonal relationships, the potential for interpersonal problems is high and is evidenced by:

- confusion, distrust and jealousy;
- incidents of discrimination, horizontal violence or bullying;
- breaches of confidentiality;
- biased judgement and poor decisions;
- inability to offer objective feedback;
- failure to act as professional role models;
- compromise of professional responsibilities and possibly a setting's reputation;
- practitioners making themselves vulnerable to accusation by others;
- possibility of disciplinary action or termination of employment;
- risk of legal action.

When early years professionals address proposed change, they need to believe that leaders and other practitioners are trustworthy, that no one will be discriminated against, that previous confidentialities will be respected and not used against them, that decisions are fair and unbiased, that any action required of them will not compromise or make them vulnerable in any way, and that they will be appropriately supported by the leader, team and relevant others.

Because of their position, roles and responsibilities, early years leaders can feel isolated and lacking in emotional support from team members. Some early years leaders have commented that ' . . . it is lonely at the top'.

I overheard my deputy inviting other staff to meet up after work but she didn't ask me. I know I shouldn't but I felt hurt and excluded.

Manager, children's services

Those leading change today have many problems to think through, decisions to take and outcomes to reflect upon. It can be tempting to turn to a trusted colleague for emotional support and understanding, and discuss inner thoughts, concerns and doubts with someone else who knows the context. Unfortunately, leaders who allow themselves to become attached to one colleague may be influenced, albeit unconsciously and unintentionally, by their emotions when having to take difficult decisions.

One team member has consistently refused to cooperate with expectations from the area supervisor, even to the point of sabotaging her setting's quality assessment. It is my responsibility to implement disciplinary measures that may include termination of employment. But I am torn, I know she has just taken out a mortgage and needs her job. I feel that knowing so much about her personal situation and problems has made it difficult for me to act professionally and in the best interests of all concerned.

Early years adviser

Blurring the boundaries between professional relationships and friendship is a potential hazard for those leading change. For example, a leader who discusses work-related issues with one particular colleague may be accused of having a favourite and being biased towards one special practitioner. The team may think that the leader will protect or side with the perceived confidante, potentially exposing the leader to possible accusations of discrimination and the confidante to bullying. Where a leader views a practitioner as a friend (or a practitioner views the leader as a friend), they may have expectations that are inappropriate, unrealistic or unprofessional in early years contexts. In addition, when friendship develops, it can be difficult for early years leaders to offer constructive and objective feedback or apply disciplinary measures if necessary.

On the other hand, leaders who treat practitioners as friends may take any criticism from team members too personally. Early years leaders have a professional responsibility to act as role models for practitioners, making it impossible to enact professional leadership while influenced by potentially unrealistic and unworkable expectations that friendship in early years settings can entail. Finally, it is important for early years leaders to appreciate that some practitioners may find efforts to foster friendship inappropriate, intrusive or creative of a hostile work environment.

Sometimes our manager comes out with the team for a drink after work, and it's okay. But we never relax until she leaves because we can't be ourselves or say what we want to in front of her . . . we never know how she might use that later. If I want to let off steam about work, I can't do it when she is there, and that is the whole point of the team going out.

Childcare worker, children's centre

Early years leaders who promote professional interpersonal relationships in settings:

- explain and talk through their role and set boundaries, clarify interpersonal expectations and establish ground rules for professional interaction;
- respond to relationship and workplace interpersonal problems immediately;
- avoid personalizing issues and disputes that arise within work and appreciate that being liked or popular is irrelevant to leading change;
- ensure that trust and confidentiality are never breached or violated, especially by discussing practitioners inappropriately with others;
- act as a professional role model in workplace relationships and avoid inappropriate socializing in or outside work.

The establishment and maintenance of appropriate professional interpersonal relationships in early years provision is a means of bringing out the best of everyone within the early years community (Department for Children, Schools and Families 2010). Moreover, those leading change appreciate that positive interpersonal relationships rely on consistent use of key interpersonal skills.

Key interpersonal skills for leading change

The term 'interpersonal skills' is used to denote a range of capabilities that people use on a day-to-day basis to communicate and interact with others, both individuals and groups, in their personal and professional lives. Interpersonal skills are the vital abilities that enable people to interact positively and effectively with others. In early years provision, sound interpersonal skills encourage connections with and among practitioners, help engage everyone with the task, encourage participation and empower everyone to contribute. Inadequate development and performance of interpersonal skills are major obstacles to competent leadership and contribute to poor quality relationships, low-level trust and respect, unwillingness to collaborate, diminished influence, reactive opposition and poor receptivity to the need for change.

Most job descriptions for the range of positions available in early years settings refer to and call for 'well-developed' or 'excellent' interpersonal skills. This generic term usually refers to a cluster of abilities that cover:

- sending and receiving messages, both verbally and non-verbally;
- listening and understanding;
- assertion;
- emotional intelligence;
- problem-solving;
- decision-making;
- negotiation;
- conflict resolution;
- teamwork;
- stress management.

How early years professionals interact and cope with others influences both the climate and efficiency in settings. Discerning early years leaders appreciate the need to develop considerable skill in these areas in order to get along with, respond to and lead others (Sharp et al. 2012). Indeed, leaders who demonstrate considerable facility with a range of interpersonal skills tend to be perceived by others as calm, trustworthy, competent, confident and influential. They are the leaders who can make change happen.

> The last coordinator came across as interested in and knowledgeable about young children, and outwardly expressed concern about doing his job well. However, some staff thought he could be difficult to get along with because he tended to criticize rather than praise us, he bickered and argued over small issues and he complained about some practitioners behind their back. His negative approach upset some of us who avoided direct contact with him where possible. The new coordinator is just the opposite, easy to get along with, encouraging, approachable and deals with issues directly with us. The atmosphere at work is completely different now.
>
> Early years educator, pre-school centre

Both early years leaders and practitioners must acquire capability in a range of interpersonal skills. However, leaders are also expected to display:

- thorough understanding of self (in relation to awareness, concept and esteem through assessment, reflection, analysis and evaluation);
- appreciation and recognition of diversity;
- ability in dialogue, debate and reflection;

- commitment to professional ethics;
- willingness to collaborate;
- capacity for creativity and innovation.

Early years leaders who are competent in such diverse interpersonal abilities find that they become more effective in motivating practitioners, supporting and helping them to achieve agreed goals, negotiating and mediating in testing situations, and ensuring that even challenging decisions are implemented. They usually find it easier to build rapport among and foster interaction between practitioners and generally are regarded as more approachable. These attributes are essential for promoting high morale and effective teamwork, especially when there is pressure for change.

Issues affecting interpersonal relationships in early years settings

Sensitive early years leaders and practitioners appreciate that certain tendencies can interfere with and impair the functioning of interpersonal skills that foster constructive interpersonal relationships at work. Johnson (2013) suggests that fear and anxiety, shyness and self-blame can become major impediments to satisfactory interpersonal relationships and workplace interaction.

Fear and anxiety are learned emotions that can motivate avoidance of certain people and situations. Many leaders experience both fear and anxiety when pressured to address complex change and the uncertainty of the unknown. However, avoidance is an unacceptable response because it does not resolve or progress the situation. A more appropriate way to manage fear and anxiety is to acknowledge and accept them as 'feelings that can be controlled', problems that can be solved, and counter them with rational thinking and assumptions. Sometimes, facing situations that produce fear and anxiety can help overcome or counteract their negative effects.

Shyness is social anxiety coupled with behavioural inhibition or poor social skills. Shy people appear overly cautious, timid, self-conscious and are easily embarrassed during interaction with others. Shyness is not an attribute that is usually associated with competent leadership. However, for early years leaders, shyness may be experienced when they are required to interact with stakeholders who are perceived as more important, powerful or knowledgeable, or in situations where they feel out of their comfort zone.

> I represented our nursery at a public meeting considering planning permission to build a fast food outlet next to us. I was almost speechless, too shy in front of the local authority officials and dignitaries, the good and the great. But somehow I summoned up the courage, knowing that if I didn't speak up, I wasn't being an advocate, and that is part of my role as leader.
>
> Manager, day nursery

Shyness can be reduced by developing greater self-confidence and self-esteem, and by improving interpersonal and social skills. When early years leaders possess high levels of self-worth, self-confidence and optimism, they are less likely to be affected by shyness with unfamiliar people or in challenging situations.

Some early years leaders have reported that they suffer from a tendency to self-blame, that is, they judge themselves to be inadequate in some way, fail to live up to own and others' expectations, feel they are not up to the challenge, that mistakes and problems are their fault or that their behaviour has not met some personal standard of excellence. Self-blame usually generates high levels of stress and consequently diminished capacity to engage in rational thinking, appropriate decision-making and constructive problem-solving. Self-blame involves a tendency to catastrophize the situation and is a product of irrational and faulty thinking.

> When I've tried to put something new in place and it does not work out as I planned, I get so angry with myself, I feel that I've let the team down . . . especially when they work so hard to do what I ask of them. Then I lose confidence and worry about whether I'll fail in other areas . . . my mind goes round in circles.
>
> Team leader, children's centre

The current reality in the early years sector is that times are testing, challenges keep coming and risks have to be taken. Nobody is perfect, everyone makes mistakes, most people are well intentioned and do the best they can with the information they have and in the situation in which they find themselves. Hindsight is a wonderful thing! Early years leaders and practitioners who suffer from a tendency to self-blame are encouraged to accept the uncertainty of life, learn to take risks, tolerate mistakes and failure, manage and express feelings appropriately and use rational self-talk to counter irrational thinking.

Key skills for interpersonal competence in early years settings

Every early years leader and practitioner needs to acquire and demonstrate considerable interpersonal competence in their work, no more so than when facing the pressures of complicated change agendas. Interpersonal competence is the foundation for the establishment of trust and confidence, and through which constructive relationships, collaborative teamwork and collective activity for change function.

Early years leaders who are regarded as interpersonally competent by practitioners exhibit, model and set professional expectations concerning the following attitudes and abilities:

- courtesy, trust and respect (setting the standards for helpfulness, support, active listening, collaboration, tolerance, commitment, acknowledgement, friendly and professional workplace climate);

- self-awareness, knowledge and understanding (setting the standards for appropriate expression of emotion, receptivity to diversity, openness, appreciation of motivation, clarity of values and thinking, lack of bias, lifelong learning);

- rapport and collaborative team relationships (setting the standards for psychological safety, communication, inclusion, enablement, empowerment, contribution, delegation, negotiation, decision-making, problem-solving, conflict resolution, ongoing relationships, networking);

- understanding of others (setting the standards for interest in and concern for others, empathy, listening, feedback, respect for individual differences and contributions, inspiration towards and commitment to vision, shared ownership, consensus, creative and flexible thinking, mentoring).

Early years leaders who personify interpersonal competence help build cooperative teams that are resilient, interdependent, integrated and harmonious and consequently effective and productive. When those leading the current change directives are interpersonally competent, they understand practitioner and team interaction patterns, needs and motivation, are alert to what is happening in settings and intervene appropriately to move practitioners and teams forward. They communicate in ways that help practitioners to understand new circumstances, demands and goals, and encourage them to think differently, bigger, more flexibly and more creatively. Through their personal energy and direction, they inspire and motivate practitioners in ways that keep them engaged, enthusiastic, committed, involved and contributing.

Early years leaders who display interpersonal competence in times of change act as an anchor for practitioners because they continually focus on and reaffirm key values, the broad vision and the shared mission, and model the competencies required. Through their communication and action, they personify requisite attributes and skills and shape the quality of interpersonal relationships on which effecting complex change depends.

Early years leaders who are regarded as interpersonally effective demonstrate capability to:

- inspire confidence in and enjoy the confidence of practitioners;
- display a genuine interest in and regard for the welfare of team members;
- empathize with practitioners' concerns, needs and motivations;
- communicate clearly to avoid misunderstanding;
- listen with an open mind, tolerate, accept and understand different viewpoints;
- believe in and strive to accomplish agreed vision and goals;
- collaborate, delegate and open up opportunities for shared leadership;
- expect and reward performance, contribution and excellence;
- maintain objectivity and exercise insightful judgement;

- champion new ideas;
- regard challenge and change as routine for quality improvement.

Closing thoughts

In times of complex change, the key to moving practice forward and enhancing quality in early years provision is effective leadership, which in turn is underpinned by the development of strong interpersonal relationships and astute interpersonal capability. Of the diverse interpersonal skills that contribute to leading change, communication is the keystone that underpins the others and it is explored in more detail in the next chapter.

5

EFFECTING CHANGE THROUGH INTERPERSONAL COMMUNICATION

The art of communication is the language of leadership.
James Humes

This chapter explores:

▶ key interpersonal communication skills for leading change;
▶ the role of emotional intelligence in effecting change;
▶ obstacles to communication about change in early years settings;
▶ conveying a clear and concise vision.

According to O'Connor (2012: 35), 'communication is the glue that holds people together, . . . the way they share ideas and feelings, . . . [and] the means they use to bond and form groups'. Indeed, interpersonal communication is the language of leadership and the key to leadership success. Numerous findings indicate that leaders spend between 70 and 90 per cent of their time in various forms of communication, with face-to-face communication being the dominant mode (Barrett 2006, 2010). However, the growing popularity and acceptance of electronic communication in early years provision, including mobile telephones, emails, instant messaging and social networking, may impact on the amount of time spent in face-to-face communication. However, regardless of the mode of communication, it is obvious that early years leaders can inspire, motivate, guide, direct and encourage others only when they communicate effectively with each practitioner and the team as a whole.

Last week I had one of those difficult conversations with a certain coordinator . . . Although she says she's on board with the changes we want to make as a team, she is stubborn and inflexible about her work. I had to find the right communication dynamic to persuade her to commit to a small change in the roster that would really help the whole team. She only wants to focus on her job and seems to find it hard to take a broader view of the setting's work.

Manager, children's services

Because change is essentially an emotional human process, leading change is a test of the effectiveness of any leader's communication skills. For early years leaders to bring practitioners on board, and nurture receptivity and readiness to implement proposed reforms and directives, they need to clarify the reasons for change, show how change proposals fit with the shared vision and present proposed changes as achievable and beneficial endeavours. Consequently, those leading change in early years settings may find that they need to persuade practitioners to endorse proposed changes, that is, they need to effectively communicate the need for and reasons behind directives in ways that help those involved appreciate, accept and actively commit to putting them into place.

Leadership has been described as a dialogue with strategic intentions that creates a cognitive and emotional closeness between leaders and practitioners, encourages deeper thinking and results in greater understanding (Deakin 2007; Dunlop 2008; Siraj-Blatchford and Hallet 2013). Early years leaders regularly need to assess and improve their expertise in interpersonal communication because it is essential for success in life and work, it helps build and maintain positive interpersonal relationships, and because it is the starting point for encouraging receptivity to and readiness for change.

The strength of our provision comes from the team. We are a great team, supportive, encouraging and productive . . . we focus on maintaining positive relationships, not friendships but good working relationships . . . then we can communicate openly about most things . . . like now with all the changes.

Team leader, children's early learning centre

Quality interpersonal relationships help early years professionals to feel connected, confident and competent to cope with challenge, pressure and stress, and in times of change they are integral to successful instigation, implementation and sustainability.

Competent leaders of change communicate in a composed and purposeful style and pace in order to transmit meaning that will influence followers and relevant others (Barrett 2010). Nothing undermines people's confidence in their ability to meet pressure for change more than ineffective and inconsistent communication between leader and team members (Kotter 2011). In fact, breakdown in interpersonal communication is one of the biggest contributors to failure to implement and embed change in the workplace.

When I read about the change agenda, I immediately knew it was up to me to interpret, translate and present it in a way that the team would accept. I really needed to think about the best way to communicate to them the work that would be required of us all so that they didn't get their backs up.

Coordinator, children's centre

When those leading change in early years settings acquire and demonstrate confidence and skill in effective interpersonal communication, they benefit from being able to:

- convey ideas, goals and plans clearly and concisely;
- get across their vision to a range of people;
- strengthen relationships within and across teams;
- enhance their personal trustworthiness and credibility;
- maximize collaboration;
- nurture and shape a positive workplace environment and culture;
- employ and model better decision-making and problem-solving strategies;
- use diversity to enhance workplace culture and productivity;
- respond to conflict in constructive ways;
- engage and motivate teams to respond positively, thereby counteracting resistance to proposed changes.

In order to act as agents of change, early years professionals depend on sophisticated expertise in interpersonal communication. Competent change agents communicate effectively across the various stakeholders who participate in and contribute to the process of introducing and implementing proposals for change. When responding to pressure for complicated change, effective communication skills are fundamental for coordinating, taking responsibility and being accountable for the completion of the different tasks and activities asked of practitioners, senior administrators and associated professionals. In addition, skilled interpersonal communication helps strengthen interconnectivity between everyone involved and supports them in managing and reducing any tension and stress associated with the challenges, pressures and possibilities that demands for change may bring.

Communicating and listening: essential skills for effecting change

Interpersonal communication is a two-way process that involves transmitting a message from one person to another in way that ensures the message is heard and understood as intended (Johnson 2013). Although it can be achieved in written and electronic forms, *interpersonal* (that is, between people) communication is most effective when undertaken face-to-face. The goal of communication is achieving understanding through the exchange of information, feelings and meaning. Effective interpersonal communication occurs in an appropriate context and is effected through the use of specific verbal and non-verbal skills that generate understanding, foster trust and encourage the commitment and participation of others.

When early years leaders communicate effectively, they improve their ability to make sound decisions and get things done with and through others (Barrett 2006), an essential facility when early years provision is under pressure to address complex change directives. Numerous authors, including O'Sullivan (2009), Sims (2011) and Rodd (2013a), examine the role and range of core communication skills relevant to early years professionals and contexts.

In relation to effecting change, the two most important communication skills for early years leaders and practitioners to develop are:

- sending accurate messages;
- active (or reflective) listening.

Sending or transmitting clear messages involves the sender encoding intended information accurately and a recipient precisely decoding, translating, interpreting and understanding the information. A message has not been communicated successfully until the recipient has understood it. Achievement of accurate understanding is influenced by content and context. Content refers to the actual words or symbols, that is, language, in the message. Unfortunately, content (such as the articulation of a proposed change and the reason for it) can be subject to a good deal of misunderstanding and misinterpretation. Context, sometimes described as 'paralinguistics', refers to non-spoken factors that influence how a message is delivered and also may be subject to considerable confusion and misunderstanding. Effective two-way communication is achieved via feedback from the recipient, which lets the sender know whether the message has been understood or not. Consequently, communication results from a clear and accurate *exchange* of information between all parties.

Johnson's (2013) suggestions are helpful for early years professionals who wish to ensure clear communication during the process of change.

- use 'I' statements to 'own' transmissions;
- include all the information necessary to make messages complete and specific;
- display congruence between verbal and non-verbal messages;
- repeat the message and use several channels or media;
- ask for and listen to feedback about how messages are received;
- re-frame and shape messages as appropriate for recipients' frame of reference;

- convey feelings and emotions, verbally and non-verbally, accurately, unambiguously and appropriately;
- describe behaviour or situations objectively without interpreting, judging or evaluating.

When early years professionals are presented with the challenge of responding to complicated change directives, they need to be particularly attentive to the messages they send to others and the way that their messages are received and interpreted.

> Since we've known about the changes that we have to make, communication seems to have deteriorated, people don't seem to be listening to me or to one another properly . . . too many times some practitioners have jumped to conclusions about what has been said or what needs to happen, and this has only caused more confusion and negativity.
>
> Head teacher, nursery school

The pressure for change can raise both senders' and recipients' stress levels, which can interfere with accurate two-way communication. Consequently, as well as attending to the clarity of their own communications, senders must also be receptive to any feedback relevant to message delivery and recipient understanding. Improving how messages are sent requires senders to listen to the recipients' responses and reactions to content and context, and use this information to modify further transmissions.

Receiving, interpreting and accurately decoding messages requires skill in attentive or active listening. According to Johnson (2013), listening is a challenging activity that is fundamental to building and maintaining constructive interpersonal relationships, and it is a skill that is highlighted in much of the literature related to leadership in early years contexts. Listening is more than simply *hearing*; it is an intentional and motivated activity where a recipient communicates to the sender that they have heard and understood the purpose and meaning of a message. Listening is an active process that involves searching for meaning, for example to acquire or verify information, to understand others and their viewpoints, to solve problems, to explore how others are feeling, to show support or to ascertain mutual interests and concerns.

It is impossible to build positive relationships if recipients do not indicate that they have listened attentively through the communication of a relevant response to senders. Careful listening conveys an implicit subtext that expresses concern about and interest in understanding what the sender is trying to communicate. Both personal and professional relationships become more aloof, unfriendly, distant, unsympathetic or even hostile when recipients do not appear to make an effort to listen and understand.

I was talking to the head on the phone, and I knew she wasn't listening to me, I could hear her tapping the computer keys and her responses to what I was saying seemed vague, she wasn't really listening. Though I couldn't see her, I could tell by the tone of conversation that she had her mind on other things.

Teacher, nursery school

As well as the ability to send clear and precise messages, it is helpful if those leading change in early years settings communicate to others that they are interested and motivated to listen and understand. Equally, in their interaction with those leading change, early years professionals must demonstrate that they are willing to put energy into listening and understanding and that they are motivated to do so. Early years practitioners who are effective listeners:

- spend more time listening than talking;
- respect and allow speakers to finish;
- ask open questions;
- do not interrupt;
- do not answer questions with questions;
- do not dominate exchanges;
- do not move the focus of the dialogue back to their interests;
- think about their reply and offer meaningful feedback after the speaker has finished.

Unfortunately, attentive or active listening is subject to a number of common obstacles, barriers or mistakes, especially when people are under pressure or stress. Typical difficulties encountered when listening include lack of attention, becoming distracted, thinking about or doing other things, filtering or ignoring certain information, thinking about and/or replying before hearing the complete message, focusing on details rather than the meaning as a whole, interpreting meaning from a biased viewpoint and evaluating the content of the message prematurely.

I can see some eyes glaze over when I ask about progress towards our set targets in staff meetings. I think this means those practitioners have cut off and don't want to talk about it. Maybe they think I will be critical but it is my responsibility to gauge the team's progress.

Director, early learning centre

When faced with demands for change, every early years professional needs to appreciate that the ability to listen for understanding may be influenced and/or impaired by personal perception, thoughts, biases, emotions and stress levels.

> When the manager called me to her office, all I could think of was 'what have I done wrong now?' At first, I thought that she was telling me I needed more training because I wasn't doing my job properly but then I realized that she was offering me an opportunity to do a course that I put my name down for ages ago. Because I was tense, I didn't hear what she was saying at first.
>
> Childcare educator, childcare centre

Especially when change is on the agenda, the type of feedback offered by early years professionals indicates whether or not they have listened and understood. As illustrated below, different forms of feedback vary in impact and outcome. Carl Rogers's seminal response alternatives (summarized by Johnson 2013) are listed below in terms of the frequency with which they occur in personal and professional interpersonal communication.

- **Evaluative** feedback is the most frequent and least helpful option because it focuses on judgement, worth, approval, disapproval, appropriateness of the message. For example, 'I don't agree with that proposal, I think you are wrong', 'this change will not help the setting', 'we tried it before and it didn't work', 'you ought to check with other coordinators to see how they are handling it'.

- **Interpretative** or paraphrasing feedback attempts to explain what the message means. For example, 'the problem with that idea is', 'we're not moving forward because' or 'you think that we can improve by'.

- **Supportive** feedback attempts to assist, bolster, buoy up or hearten the sender. For example, 'we tried, that's the best we can do', 'the day will run more smoothly when we get used to the new regime' or 'don't worry, change is always difficult, it'll come good in the end'.

- **Probing** feedback uses closed and open questions to gather additional information, to discuss, analyse or clarify a statement. Closed questions can appear threatening and critical, for example, 'did you change the rota?' or 'don't you agree with that proposal?' Open-ended questions usually result in more elaborate information, for example, 'what did the families think about the proposal?', 'where to from here?', 'how did the team handle the additional record-keeping?' or 'who do we know with expertise in that area?'

- **Understanding** feedback tries to explore, uncover, discover and comprehend the complete meaning of the message. It is the most helpful but least frequently used response in interpersonal communication. For example, 'we're feeling discouraged because our funding submission wasn't successful', 'you're confident that if we work at it, we'll make the progress we want' or 'you don't seem convinced that we are meeting the standards expected'.

In themselves, the response alternatives are acceptable for a variety of situations. However, especially when faced with the pressure for change, the over-use of the evaluative option compared to the others and, in particular, the under-use of the understanding alternative diminishes the quality of interpersonal communication and consequently relationships.

> Some team members are ready to criticize before they have had time to think about what is being said.
>
> Teacher, nursery school

Early years professionals who are effective communicators devote energy and effort to trying to accurately understand what others want to communicate before evaluating or judging what is being said. It is the understanding response that implicitly conveys to the sender that the listener cares about, is interested in and motivated to understand the message's intended meaning, and it also encourages the sender to elaborate on and extend the communication. This type of response is particularly relevant when discussing proposed changes.

Successful leadership of complex change in early years provision requires a number of additional communication skills.

- **Assertion** – ability, based in the belief of the individual right to make a confident and positive statement or expression of information, personal perspective or feeling in a manner that does not impact upon the rights and self-esteem of others.

- **Decision-making** – ability to identify and weigh up information and evidence to make an appropriate choice and take responsibility for its impact and outcome.

- **Delegation** – ability to identify when and with whom to share the responsibility for undertaking certain tasks and decisions (as well as genuine distribution of collective authority and responsibility).

- **Negotiation** – ability to talk, confer and work with practitioners to influence them to reach an acceptable agreement or settle an issue, usually involving some 'give and take' to reach compromise or consensus.

- **Problem-solving** – ability to work through the details of a dilemma, option or difficulty to reach the best solution possible with the information and resources at hand.

Because pressure for complex change may generate significant emotional reactions in those affected by it, competence in conflict resolution and reducing stress is also essential for successfully initiating, implementing and leading complex change (Sharp et al. 2012). However, because these reactions are closely related to resisting change, such skills will be covered separately in Chapter 6.

Emotional intelligence and leading change   ←   *look up Goleman.*

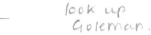

As well as skill in sending and receiving messages, effective leaders of change display high levels of emotional intelligence. Goleman (2002) argues that emotional intelligence accounts for 85 per cent of what separates top leaders from average performers. According to Goleman (1996), emotional intelligence refers to emotional and social knowledge, and the ability to:

* be aware of, understand and express oneself;
* be aware of, understand and relate to others;
* control and express strong emotions authentically and appropriately;
* show flexibility in responding to interpersonal problems;
* react positively and adapt to change.

Without emotional intelligence, those leading change in early years settings are unlikely to effectively communicate with, guide and direct others because they lack the ability to interpret and translate the emotions of self and others into flexible relevant action. Emotionally intelligent early years leaders make fewer communication errors because they understand the context and audience, a skill that is especially important when faced with proposed changes. Therefore, they are able to select the most appropriate medium for clarity of transmission, thus ensuring accurate understanding by recipients. Emotional intelligence allows those leading change to understand what motivates others to listen and act, and therefore helps them understand how to gain the commitment and contribution of practitioners for realizing a vision.

Emotional intelligence is an attribute that has long been viewed as fundamental to leadership in early years contexts (O'Sullivan 2007; Siraj-Blatchford and Hallet 2013). In times of change, capability in emotional intelligence allows change leaders to connect meaningfully with practitioners and use their interpersonal skills to enhance the development of supportive professional relationships and collaborative teamwork (Bruno 2008).

In addition, emotional intelligence helps those leading change to select the most effective medium and style for transmitting messages, thereby ensuring that communication is accurately and unambiguously sent and received, and any detrimental effects arising from misinterpretation and misunderstanding can be avoided or at least minimized. In times of complex change, when accurate two-way communication underpins goal attainment and progress, the ability to connect with practitioners on an appropriate

look up this book

emotional level enhances the trustworthiness and credibility of change leaders and consequently their influence.

Emotionally intelligent early years professionals usually have high moral standards and a well-developed sense of professional ethics (Kremenitzer and Miller 2008). Effective interpersonal communication by early years leaders is underpinned by the personification of professional values and ethics in their personality and behaviour. They 'walk the talk', that is, what they do is consistent with what they say. If those leading change are perceived as trustworthy, honest, knowledgeable, courageous and ethical, and act that way, they are more able to persuade and influence practitioners to commit to a vision and path of action for reform and quality improvement. Ethical early years leaders are perceived as having greater depth and substance and consequently inspire confidence in others, which is particularly important when faced with today's complex change directives.

When those leading change in early years provision possess high levels of emotional intelligence, they strengthen the quality of interpersonal communication because they are able to assess people and situations accurately, and select the most appropriate form, style and medium for the context and recipients. Consequently, they are less likely to suffer from any misunderstanding, conflict about, and opposition to, proposals for change that occur as a result of poor communication.

Roadblocks to effective communication in early years settings

The process of interpersonal communication is extremely complex and consequently vulnerable to miscommunication, confusion and misunderstanding. Complications and misinterpretations arise from interferences, intrusions and interruptions in the process of transmission and reception of messages. Such difficulties arise from issues with the sender, receiver and within the context. Early years leaders of change who are effective communicators anticipate, avoid and plan for potential breakdown or roadblocks in communication. They employ a range of strategies to facilitate accurate transmission and reception of messages as well as address contextual factors that impinge on successful interpersonal communication.

The most common roadblocks to effective communication arise from:

- features of the physical environment, including inappropriate time, place, distance, space, noise, atmosphere and other distractions;
- poor choice of medium for the content or situation, including written, verbal, non-verbal, visual, in person, non-face-to-face;
- semantics, due to varied connotative meanings in words and phrases;
- culture and diversity;
- psychological factors, including attitudes, moods, relationships, emotions;
- varying perceptions of reality due to differences in understanding, comprehension and frames of reference;
- workplace structures, systems and communication channels.

Factors that affect early years professionals' ability to transmit clear and concise communications about change include:

- imparting messages in unsuitable contexts;
- lack of understanding about the recipient;
- lack of dexterity with specific skills and their appropriate usage;
- projecting an artificial or false personal image;
- using the wrong medium;
- poor timing;
- ignoring ethical factors impinging on appropriate and accurate transmission.

Early years professionals who send clear and understandable messages think about and prepare for communication by clarifying the purpose or goal, thinking about and selecting the most efficient medium (for example, in person, in writing, one-to-one, in a group), and anticipating receivers' feelings, viewpoints and reactions. They recognize that their style of delivery conveys other subtexts, for example conviction, importance or urgency. They also confirm that the message was understood accurately and as intended before moving on to further communications.

> I know that some of the team prefer and benefit more from a one-to-one to talk about how they could work differently and better.
>
> Coordinator, pre-school centre

Effective communicators about proposed change in early years settings ensure that their messages are clear and understandable. Straightforward and concise messages help reduce any uncertainty or anxiety in recipients generated by unexpected or unanticipated change proposals. Recipients who decode transmitted messages through a haze of uncertainty or anxiety are more likely to misunderstand and misinterpret the content of those messages.

Factors that affect accurate understanding of a message in the often emotionally charged atmosphere surrounding change initiatives include:

- muddled, unclear, illogical, ambiguous messages;
- lack of respect and empathy by the sender;
- inappropriate or offensive tone and style of delivery;
- failure to identify the purpose or key points of the message;
- dissonance between conflicting emotions or thoughts;
- misunderstanding from cultural or language differences;
- prejudice, stereotypes and a closed mind;
- questionable values or unethical subtext.

Early years professionals' ability to interpret and understand messages accurately and as intended is enhanced when they respect the sender, keep an open mind, pay attention to verbal content and body language, and communicate their own understanding of a message's purpose and content.

Other commonplace roadblocks to effective communication about change can include:

- the use of jargon, colloquialisms, abbreviations, acronyms, unfamiliar terms and over-complicated messages;
- unfamiliar accents or dialects;
- expectations based on stereotypes and prejudices;
- tackling and avoiding taboo subjects;
- poor retention due to information overload, inattention or lack of respect or motivation;
- manipulation of or withholding information to make the overall message more positive and acceptable;
- conflict about, opposition and resistance to change;
- tension and stress.

Given that roadblocks exist and misunderstandings arise with considerable frequency in communication about change, face-to-face contact can offer important benefits for overcoming potential difficulties.

> After we talked about the proposal, I picked up from a facial expression that, though she told me she agreed, she still wasn't comfortable with taking on some different tasks. So, I took a risk, and asked her about that feeling. I knew if I didn't sort it out, she could trash what we'd discussed with other staff and I didn't want that to happen.
>
> Coordinator, nursery centre

Despite the increasing reliance on electronic communication in the early years sector, the medium cannot replace face-to-face interaction. In relation to change, face-to-face communication offers important interpersonal benefits that promote social bonding, team connectivity, commitment to vision and motivation to act. Electronic communication can become a roadblock if it creates interpersonal distance between stakeholders or fails to generate connectivity, commitment and action. Face-to-face communication about proposed change helps early years professionals to develop essential trust, connection and community, and opens access to fuller meaning via essential non-verbal information, thereby reducing the possibility of misunderstanding.

Sometimes I think that younger (and also not so young) staff text me because they cannot face telling me something in person . . . texting that they are sick when they really want time off for non-work activity. They try to avoid any negative reaction I might have . . . and that is being irresponsible. I usually confront them later, so they have to communicate directly with me. Eventually they learn it's better to tell me in person.

Coordinator, childcare centre

In addition, certain subject matter is better handled through face-to-face communication, for example delegation, negotiation, delicate issues (such as disciplinary situations) and complex information (such as that involved in proposed change). Face-to-face communication is more appropriate when those leading change have to explain their rationale for decisions and assess the reactions of, or negotiate with, team members. Face-to-face communication helps reduce the potential for conflict because understanding can be clarified, concerns acknowledged and objections countered. Consequently, face-to-face communication creates a synergy that encourages faster innovative thinking, consensual decision-making and problem-solving. Although electronic communication might appear to save time and effort, in some situations five minutes of face-to-face communication can be more efficient than a round of emails back and forth between parties.

Early years settings offer a range of opportunities for effective face-to-face communication about change, including team meetings, information sessions, round-table discussions, specific problem-solving sessions, feedback meetings, consultation forums, outreach meetings and conferences. Such face-to-face occasions give those leading change a window and time to explain the reasons behind change, crystallize the vision, provide more detail, elaborate on plans and strategies, acknowledge any negative reactions from stakeholders, respond to rumours, concede potentially unfavourable outcomes and acknowledge that they do not have all the answers. It is also essential to maintain positive attitudes and demeanour in face-to-face communication and not become distracted by any negativity concerning proposed changes.

Early years leaders and practitioners who are skilled communicators appreciate that misunderstandings are common and interference in interpersonal exchanges can be encountered at any stage in communication processes. Therefore, they plan to overcome and minimize any roadblocks, thus avoiding unintended outcomes and wasted time in communication exchanges. Roadblocks act as filters that impede and distort clarity and understanding. Therefore, competence in active listening and face-to-face communication is essential to surmount factors that can impede effective interpersonal communication.

Communicating the vision for change

Vision animates, inspires and transforms purpose into action.
Warren Bennis

Begin with the end in mind.
Stephen Covey (2004)

The process of change starts with vision, that is, an idea or concept about the future. Vision for change is 'the big picture' that ignites energy and motivation, channels strategies and action plans and paints the beneficial outcomes of successfully implementing change directives. Vision is the focal point of the motivating energy that engages and enlists early years professionals' commitment and support. Vision inspires and promotes the idea of a better future, which in turn ignites the energy needed to drive change forward. A clearly communicated vision encourages early years professionals to buy into it because it also spells out 'what's in it for me', the potential benefits for those affected by proposed change. A clear vision is a statement about commitment to the pursuit of excellence; it makes sense of and gives meaning to pressure for change and offers direction for and encouragement of those involved.

Those who lead change effectively in early years provision communicate a vision statement that outlines hopes, plans and potential benefits of an improved future to practitioners, teams and related professionals. Very simply, a vision for change is a compelling picture of a desired future that, when properly communicated, fires up early years practitioners' willingness to support it, work for it and in some way help to achieve it. A vision for change is the starting point for developing action plans for transforming ideas into reality. Ideally, both vision and action plans are co-created by everyone concerned with proposed change. When early years practitioners participate in creating the vision and developing the action plans that scaffold it, they experience a sense of *ownership*. Ownership stimulates dedication to moving forward and motivation to overcome any difficulties that may be encountered during the implementation process.

Ownership is forged by genuine respectful conversations between early years leaders, practitioners and other stakeholders. Two-way communication and ongoing dialogue are key functions for effecting change because they help:

- ease transitions through the process;
- clarify uncertainty and ambiguity;
- transform pessimism into optimism;
- shift critics from a perspective of loss to one of benefit;
- motivate sceptics to let go of the old and embrace the new;

- empower practitioners to fight for what they believe in and counter detractors;
- re-orient those clinging to an outmoded past to the future;
- acknowledge and validate endings to allow access to beginnings;
- frame change as a process and journey rather than an ordained route to a destination.

When early years practitioners talk freely about their concerns, feel listened to, understood and respected, and think that those leading change directives take their opinions seriously, they become more amenable towards implementing action plans.

> The director always gives us time in meetings to bring up our concerns and worries about the new ways of working, although sometimes it is hard to be honest in front of the whole team. But her office is always open and she usually finds time to have a coffee and a personal chat about how the changes might affect me in the future. I think that is why we trust and respect her so much.
>
> Teacher, early learning centre

A vision for an improved future should pinpoint and highlight the relevant professional values and goals that underpin and ground proposed change. Early years practitioners who appreciate how professional ethics and goals relate to the vision for change are more likely to value and contribute to the process regardless of any doubts or ambivalence that may be encountered during implementation.

Kotter (2012) agues that the likelihood of change initiatives failing to become reality is related to three fundamental leadership miscalculations:

- underestimating the power of vision for change;
- under-communicating the vision to others; and
- allowing communication difficulties to cloud or distort the vision.

Therefore, those leading change directives for quality improvement in early years settings need to articulate a concise and explicit vision that is:

- imaginable and conceivable;
- desirable and appealing;
- focused and clear;
- open and candid;
- unambiguous, uncomplicated and understandable;
- feasible, realistic and do-able.

Early years practitioners will be more receptive to vision for change that is brief, for example the main points outlined in about half a page or verbally reviewed in a couple of minutes. Any longer and practitioners might become bored, lose track, and their minds may start to wander back to more pressing day-to-day issues and concerns. It is important for those leading change in early years settings to carefully think about and plan when and how best to communicate a vision regarding proposed change. Otherwise, a valuable opportunity to attract practitioners' interest and commitment to the 'big picture' direction and plans for change can be lost.

In early years settings, a vision for change is created and built on the communication of shared values and inspiration about the possibilities and shape of an improved future. In communicating a compelling vision, those leading change act as intentional change agents who possess power to influence positive outcomes for quality improvement in early years provision. Those who successfully lead change appreciate that persuasive communication encourages understanding, understanding generates acceptance, which in turn brings about action (Garvin and Roberto 2011). Effective leadership of change in early years provision is built upon convincing communication, guidance and transformation of ideas, innovation and policies focused on action by and with practitioners and relevant others.

Closing thoughts

Pressure for change can give rise to communication difficulties between those concerned at a time when honesty and clarity are of utmost importance. Effective interpersonal communication during the process of change is dependent upon leaders' ability to transmit open, respectful and transparent messages using formats and media appropriate to the context and recipients, the initiation of respectful reciprocal conversations and dialogue grounded in listening, reflection and consultation, and the development of communication dynamics that encourage everyone concerned with change proposals to question, suggest, debate, interpret, negotiate, review, verify and confirm received understanding. Clear interpersonal communication can counter any feelings of tension, anxiety and stress arising from demands for change as well as perceived endangerment to personal well-being, professional identity and existing competence. It can can help generate the high level of trust required for taking the inevitable chances, possibilities and risks inherent in making visions and proposals for change happen.

6

FROM REACTIVE OPPOSITION TO PROACTIVE RECEPTIVITY TO CHANGE

If you want to make enemies, try to change something.
Woodrow Wilson

This chapter explores:

▶ the nature of opposition and resistance;
▶ the process of adjusting to change;
▶ strategies for managing stress during change;
▶ typical reactions to conflict;
▶ strategies for channelling resistance into commitment;
▶ promoting receptivity to change.

One of the greatest tests for those leading change is to identify and overcome opposition, conflict and resistance (Heifitz and Linsky 2011). Negative reactions to proposed change come in many forms and with different levels of intensity, and those leading change need to find creative ways of overcoming them (Whalley and Allen 2011). The early years sector has experienced pressure for change in the past. However, many authors report an observed tendency towards reactive negativity, opposition or resistance (Ebbeck and Waniganayake 2003; Miller and Cable 2011; Stamopoulos 2011; Whalley and Allen 2011; Elliot 2012). In fact, the Unison *Newsletter for Early Years Workers* (Unison in Early Years 2013) reports that the raft of changes proposed for early years provision in England have been met with 'almost universal criticism' and that over 50,000 people had already signed petitions to oppose the changes.

The phenomena of opposition and resistance

Opposition, expressed as objection and dissent in argument or action, can be reactive, that is, arguing or acting in response to proposed change, rather than instigating or influencing it proactively. More intense conflict about proposed change is evidenced through disagreement, quarrels or confrontation, and usually arises from anxiety about and perceived threats to personal and professional needs, concerns, interests and identity, differing views about how the processes should be handled, or challenges to the authority and power of those leading it.

Resistance is displayed by refusal to accept or comply with change, or by attempting to prevent change happening. This is a common and well-documented phenomenon in early years provision that may be a product of practitioners' beliefs about and prior experience with change. It may not be the proposed change itself that produces negativity, opposition and resistance. Sometimes, it is early years practitioners' perceptions about proposed changes that determine whether these are viewed as a burden or threat (and consequently to be argued, opposed and resisted) or a challenging opportunity for learning and growth (and therefore to be welcomed and embraced). Few experiences elicit such intense emotional reaction in human beings, including early years professionals, as does the prospect of change.

Consequently, one of the most demanding responsibilities of those leading change in early years settings is transforming reactive opposition into proactive receptivity to new ideas and ways of working, that is, encouraging early years practitioners to be ready in advance to accept and respond to anticipated or even unexpected proposals for change. Whalley and Allen (2011) suggest that, when those leading change in early years provision understand why some practitioners react negatively to change, they can work with them to address specific concerns and help them to see the positive aspects of engaging with it.

Emotionally intelligent leaders of change in early years settings appreciate that individual practitioners react differently to the experience of stability and change in life and work. Some practitioners prefer certainty and steadiness. They like the way things have been and are. Other practitioners prefer that circumstances change periodically or occasionally become different; they enjoy uncertainty, possibility, are interested in novelty and are excited by looking for the new or unfamiliar. Problems may arise when early years practitioners find themselves in circumstances that are not their preference, for example when a stability-oriented practitioner experiences pressure for rapid or ongoing change or a change-oriented practitioner is bored by constant and unvarying circumstances. Reactions to both of these positions can be mild, strong or intense and may be expressed as dissatisfaction, stress, negativity, irrationality, opposition and resistance.

Many people, including early years professionals, argue about, oppose and resist change because they fear being pushed out of their comfort zone, that they will experience feelings of inadequacy or that in some way pressure for change will be detrimental to their well-being and future. The current agenda for reform in the early years sector asks early years professionals to change their thinking, adjust their practice, improve their skills, demonstrate enhanced performance, and thereby improve the quality of early years provision. While some early years practitioners regard such aims as a normal part of their professional responsibilities, others have interpreted them as threats to their current self-concept and self-esteem, that is, threats to their stability and personal comfort zone.

Despite the availability of literature, training and development options and opportunities for ongoing professional dialogue abut change-based quality improvement within the sector, some early years professionals remain anxious, suspicious about and reluctant to pursue new possibilities and pathways. This is not because they are not interested in quality improvement. Rather, some early years practitioners feel uncomfortable about or lack confidence to take risks because they feel more secure with what they experience as familiar and known. Since the current change agenda became public, numerous early years leaders have commented about increased frequency in gossip, rumour and hushed conversations among staff members.

> I wouldn't say that I am cynical about the proposed changes but having worked in this sector for over twenty years, let's just say, I've seen and heard it all before. We get all worked up about implementing some new idea and then before we know it, they think up something else for us.
>
> Early years educator, pre-school centre

The current change directives have not been greeted with unanimous enthusiasm. Some early years professionals continue to express increasing anxiety about the scope, magnitude and pace of change that they are expected to address and integrate into practice. Others claim that they are weary and exhausted from having to respond to what they perceive as 'the perpetual and unrelenting pressure from above' to implement directives for change. Anxiety about personal ability to respond to proposed change increases the likelihood of stress, conflict and resistance: the greater the anxiety and stress, the greater the probability of opposition, conflict and resistance. While many early years leaders and practitioners continue to strive to meet expectations, some have reacted negatively, perceiving and dismissing change directives in defeatist ways.

> I know a number of early years directors who are struggling on – fighting the noble fight – to meet the statutory requirements – it is only their personal determination and resolve not to be defeated that keeps them going in the face of gloomy responses from staff.
>
> Professional development trainer, early years department

Given the constancy, rapidity and degree of change within the early years sector, it is no longer professionally acceptable to harbour suspicion about or act arbitrarily to oppose, obstruct or prevent change. Moreover, apathy about change can lead to complacency with a concomitant desire to preserve the status quo and personal comfort zone. Early years professionals benefit from encouragement and support from those leading change to re-channel any negative tendencies into positive, proactive, future-oriented attitudes and action concerning appropriate proposals.

Unfortunately, both literature and experience indicate that the greater the complexity of change, the greater the probability that it will be met with argument, opposition, challenge and resistance from those affected by it. In relation to the current change agenda, early years practitioners are more likely to be negative about, oppose and resist change directives when they:

- can't see the big picture – the why, where or how proposed change fits in;
- are satisfied with and want to preserve the status quo;
- genuinely believe change to be inappropriate for children and settings;
- perceive the risks associated with change as too great, either personally or professionally;
- feel that their opinions, concerns and feelings are not heard, respected or considered;
- do not perceive genuine benefits for staff, children, families, local communities or the sector;
- are not meaningfully involved in design and development processes;
- lack confidence about their ability to implement different or new ways of working;
- have no or poor role models for new ways of working;
- lack confidence in leadership;
- lack trust in or object to 'top-down' or externally imposed change proposals;
- feel overloaded and overwhelmed by the scope, magnitude and timing, lacking in support and time to adjust to and implement change;
- think that other factors need changing more urgently.

The most common reasons early years professionals oppose and resist change include fear of the unknown, fear of loss of security, power or status, lack of trustworthy and/or relevant information, absence of compelling reasons, lack of resources, poor timing and desire to maintain that which is familiar, routine and habitual. However, not all resistance to change is subjective, emotional and reactive; sometimes resistance is grounded in professional, objective and rational beliefs and reservations (National Union of Teachers 2013). Those leading change in early years settings need to appreciate the emotional and professional factors that may influence opposition and resistance and take them into account when initiating, discussing or addressing proposed change with practitioners.

Moving from shock to adjustment

There are few experiences that ignite strong emotions as does change, and early years professionals are not immune to intense emotional reaction where change is concerned. While some respond to pressure for change with enthusiasm and involvement and others respond with complete apathy, some early years professionals experience various forms of negative reaction, including scepticism, cynicism, hurt, fear, anger, helplessness, defeat, frustration and resentment. Anecdotal evidence from early years leaders indicates that some practitioners display significantly negative emotional reactions when discussing what the current change directives mean for them and their setting. These reactions appear to be similar to Elizabeth Kübler-Ross's stages of grieving (Kübler-Ross and Kessler 2005) and illustrate how some of those affected by proposed change in the early years sector move from an initial state of uncomprehending shock through to final acceptance and adjustment to the new order.

- Shock and initial disbelief – 'It won't happen!'
- Denial and fear – 'It's not happening!'
- Anger and resentment – 'It won't happen if I can help it!'
- Apathy and depression – 'I'll lose so much when it happens!'
- Acceptance – 'If it's going to happen then I might as well get on with it!'
- Adjustment and accommodation to the new reality because it works well, has resulted in obvious improvements or has given a new sense of purpose – 'Actually, it's okay, things seem to work better since we made those changes!'

When transitioning through the first three stages, there are tipping points where early years practitioners meet the possibility of moving from the negative towards the positive, for example from perceptions of loss to safety, from doubt to certainty and from apprehension to motivation. The tipping point for these practitioners comes when genuine empathic support from those leading change tilts the balance towards the positive. Empathic change leaders appreciate the importance of responding to practitioners' evident confusion, anxiety, uncertainty and disorientation. This helps those worried about change to move to a more neutral position where they can begin to come to terms with and accept demands for change. If acceptance does not occur, the ongoing frustration experienced by those affected by proposed change may eventually lead to lethargy, apathy and withdrawal.

It is only when practitioners acknowledge that they are at the cusp of a new beginning that positive emotions such as excitement and enthusiasm become the motivation and energy required to drive change forward. Those leading change in early years settings, who appreciate that much conflict and resistance results from perceived threat to personal comfort zones, will offer sufficient psychological protection that supports practitioners to move into a more confident, optimistic, cooperative and integrated state of mind about change.

Empathic early years leaders understand that everyone has fundamental personal needs that have to be met in order to feel confident and competent. In relation to complicated change, these needs include (Schutz 1994):

- the need for control over one's environment and future;
- the need for inclusion in the process of change;
- the need for openness from those leading and responsible for executing change.

Aigner (2011) suggests that perceptive leaders meet such needs by making sense of, bringing order to and providing psychological protection for team members during times of change. However, early years practitioners' expectations in relation to personal needs have to be addressed sensitively yet realistically by those leading change. During the process of change, especially with regard to mandatory directives, it may not always be possible to have control over one's work situation. Nevertheless, thoughtful early years leaders usually can find some way of ensuring that practitioners feel included and share appropriate information as transparently as possible. It is essential that those leading change in early years provision respond genuinely to practitioners' anxieties, concerns and objections as soon as they are identified or raised.

Reducing stress in times of change

Change is an inevitable fact of life and work and, whether change is perceived and approached positively or negatively, it usually generates some emotional reaction in those affected by it. Those who embrace change as a stimulating opportunity tend to experience more positive emotions, but for those who hold negative perceptions, change can produce emotions that range from minor discomfort to incapacitating levels of fear, anxiety and stress. Any change that is easily and quickly adapted to usually produces minimal stress. However, for some, change can be a powerful stressor because it is associated with feeling out of control and overwhelmed by what is happening in our environment. The more rapid and complex the change, the greater the probability that high levels of emotion and stress will be experienced. Such factors may contribute to and explain the current high turnover of senior staff and directors in children's provision in England (Puffett 2013).

The most effective way to help early years professionals cope with change-induced stress is to ensure that they participate in and have some control over how the change affects them. Insightful early years leaders appreciate the importance of including and involving every practitioner in the processes of change as a way to build support for change, reduce conflict about it and overcome resistance to it. However, other strategies that can help early years professionals cope with change-induced stress include:

- connecting with other practitioners and developing support networks with colleagues, families and friends;
- expressing feelings and talking about change openly, assertively and respectfully;
- confronting and dealing with rational and irrational anxieties and concerns;
- maintaining a positive sense of self-esteem by setting realistic and achievable expectations of self and others;
- having the courage to engage with and take control of change;
- remaining positive about change and not exaggerating any negative aspects;
- accepting changes that are inevitable and unavoidable, and not wasting energy on unproductive resistance;
- accepting that stress is a result of personal response to change and, if the situation cannot be altered, modifying personal perceptions about it and reaction to it by re-framing negatives into positives;
- taking care of physical health by ensuring adequate nutrition, sleep, relaxation, exercise and avoiding alcohol, nicotine and other drugs.

In times of change, stress may be reduced when early years professionals learn to identify what triggers their own strong emotional reactions, how stress affects them personally, how to manage emotions intelligently and react professionally when faced with stressors, and how and when to take control of the situation. It is important to understand that, if nothing else, early years practitioners have control over how they react to and allow directives for change to affect them. Although people vary in stress tolerance levels, everyone can learn to recognize their personal triggers for and reactions to stress, and develop skills to manage and reduce it.

Common reactions to conflict about change

Conflict is a common occurrence in early years provision that arises from disagreements with the leader and between practitioners because of perceived or genuine threats to needs, interests and concerns (Aubrey 2011). Different types and levels of disagreement (for example, arising from subjective, objective, minor or major perceived threats) generate different levels of emotional reaction, from less intense feelings of annoyance through to full apoplectic anger and rage. In addition, what began as a small disagreement can escalate into a major conflict because some practitioners, whether a situation affects them or not, 'take sides' based on perception of current and past issues and relationships, as well as their roles and positions within settings. Consequently, conflict in early years provision has the potential to be very emotional, complicated and testing for all involved.

There are a number of commonly observed reactions to conflict scenarios in early years settings, some of which are more appropriate and successful than others.

- **Competition:** focuses on meeting one's own needs at the expense of others' needs and controlling others, usually involving aggressive communication, little respect for others and relationships, and the use of power over others ('It's my way or the highway!'). Rather than move towards acceptable solutions, a competitive approach increases the level of threat, emotional responses and consequently the conflict.

- **Accommodation:** where one practitioner gives up their own needs to maintain relationships and thereby reach solutions ('Whatever!'). Although the needs of the team or situation are given priority, individual practitioners often end up feeling used and abused by others, with their ongoing unmet needs provoking later frustration, resentment and hostility.

- **Avoidance:** associated with a negative attitude to conflict, where feelings and viewpoints are not expressed ('I don't want to talk about it!'), resulting in the conflict festering and growing irritation, frustration, anger and bitterness. Eventually, the conflict becomes too difficult to ignore, with unsuccessful avoidance fuelling explosive, aggressive outbursts that continue and possibly escalate the conflict.

- **Compromise:** where practitioners give up something to get something through bargaining, negotiating and brokering ('I'll do X, if you do Y'). However, compromise tends to be an unsatisfactory experience for most team members. It does not achieve a win-win solution because practitioners can remain entrenched in their own positions and understandings, the level of trust remains low, willingness to cooperate is low and the probability of creative solution is diminished.

- **Collaboration:** where practitioners willingly pool their ideas and resources to work towards finding a mutually acceptable solution ('Let's work it out together!'). Collaborative approaches to conflict resolution rely on high levels of trust, open and assertive communication and cooperation. Collaborative or 'win-win' solutions respect and integrate the needs of all concerned, validate and listen to the viewpoints of all team members, incorporate the ideas of a greater number of contributors and are more likely to achieve meaningful and consensual solutions. A growing sense of respect for and goodwill towards team members is an important outcome of this approach.

Emotionally intelligent leaders in early years provision employ a range of strategies and tactics to resolve conflict about proposed change. They generally adopt a collaborative, 'win-win' approach that encourages practitioners to relinquish adversarial positions and choose more cooperative attitudes. Such leaders help those concerned to focus on underlying needs regarding proposed changes, acknowledge and respect individual differences in perspective, adapt viewpoints in the light of dialogue and information, and concentrate on issues not personalities.

Although some early years professionals find it uncomfortable, conflict is a normal event and common experience in early years settings (Ebbeck and Waniganayake 2003). The most productive approach to conflict is to define it as a collective opportunity and responsibility for creative problem-solving and learning. Given the challenging nature of some of the current directives for change, conflict should be anticipated, predicted and expected as a routine aspect of the process. Insightful early years leaders appreciate that if conflict can be transformed into a collaborative learning experience, it can become a source of energy, creativity and innovation for change. However, if conflict is not addressed constructively, it can become a problematic source of resistance to and obstruction of efforts to initiate and implement change proposals.

Strategies for channelling opposition into commitment

Although opposition and resistance can be regarded as obstacles to change, they are not necessarily so. Those who oppose and resist change possess considerable passion and energy, which is simply directed towards holding back and prevention. However, if those leading change are empathic and perceptive, they can transform this energy and passion into a fuel for dialogue, which can encourage insight and drive improvement. Discerning leaders grasp the source of opposition and adopt strategies that help to counteract and channel negative energy into positive action.

Kotter and Schlesinger (Schermerhorn et al. 2005) outlined six different strategies for overcoming opposition and resistance to change, which have been endorsed by many experts in this area. The focus, advantages and limitations of each of the strategies are outlined below.

Education and communication is beneficial where early years practitioners lack information or possess inaccurate information and analysis. This strategy helps to raise awareness about the need for and reasons behind change directives through dialogue, debate and input of information and facts, usually prior to the design and implementation stages. It can be useful where there is ignorance or inadequate awareness, where goals are not yet clearly determined and for change that may be complex or controversial. Communication of information and ideas can help early years leaders and practitioners to see the need and reason behind, the logic and sense of, and benefits of proposed change.

Continually questioning, talking about and looking at what we are doing, how we can improve our practice is essential . . . hard, time consuming but essential.
Pre-school teacher, childcare centre

Education and communication is particularly helpful during the initiation stage and works best when positive relationships exist between resisters and those early years leaders who are responsible for educating and communicating. Once practitioners fully appreciate and understand the necessity for change, they usually commit to its implementation. However, education and communication does require considerable time and effort from those leading change, which can be a major drawback where time constraints exist or many people are involved.

Participation and involvement is useful for situations when those leading change do not have all of the necessary information to plot the 'how' of change, when the design and implementation of change proposals are dependent upon the inclusion and collaboration of potential resisters, and when practitioners have considerable power to resist. When early years professionals feel a sense of connection to and ownership of proposed changes, they are more likely to support and less likely to resist them. In early years provision, participation heightens commitment.

> I know that Fran has a lot of support from and consequently power within the team, so when I need to delegate some of the additional work that the reform agenda has created, I make sure that she is on my list. That way, she works with the changes, not against them . . . and she helps bring others on board.
>
> Manager, early learning centre

Because complicated change has many facets and competent leadership in early years settings is not a solo act, it makes sense to include and involve practitioners in both its design and implementation. When early years professionals see that their input has been integrated into action plans, they are more likely to commit to implementation. Unfortunately, this strategy is also very time consuming and can result in poor solutions if practitioners do not possess sufficient knowledge and expertise or are not properly supervised and coordinated. In addition, if a change proposal requires immediate implementation, it can take too long for those leading it to appropriately involve team members. They will have to take immediate action by themselves.

Facilitation and support are most beneficial when fear, anxiety and stress are major sources of resistance. Most early years leaders appreciate that being supportive is an important part of their day-to-day responsibility to practitioners, not only when times are difficult. However, when faced with demands for complex change, some early years practitioners need increased support and help to adjust to and meet new challenges. Support can be emotional, by listening to, acknowledging and validating anxiety and concerns, and modelling stress management techniques.

I know my team is worried about being assessed. I know some of them need additional training to meet the standards and they resent it. I try to tune into their anxieties, even if they don't actually tell me about it, I think that just letting them know that I've heard how they feel helps them feel better.

Manager, childcare centre

Support can include training in new skills and allocation of time to undertake and complete tasks. Because some early years practitioners take more time than others to adjust to change, this approach can be very time consuming for those leading it. Considerable time and patience may be needed to see improvement. In addition, employment of external counsellors, mentors or coaches can be expensive. Although facilitation and support is the best approach for responding to early years practitioners' emotional and adjustment issues, it may not be the most practical and efficient approach.

Negotiation and agreement can focus on overcoming practitioner resistance through dialogue, debate and consultation to achieve agreement. Alternatively, it can mean brokering a deal by bargaining with or offering incentives to active and passive resisters, especially those who may lose out due to some aspect of change. Most early years professionals are familiar with the processes of professional dialogue and consultation and will move to agreement when they appreciate the positive aspects and benefits of proposed change, especially given the power of the 'what's in it for me' factor.

In relation to negotiating as brokering a deal, early years leaders have few incentives that they can offer, for example higher wages, time in lieu, promotion or sacrificing salary for other benefits. Regrettably, incentives usually persuade resisters to comply with, rather than commit to, the aspirations and goals of those leading change. Compliance can easily be transformed back into resistance if incentives lose their power or resisters demand more. In addition, offering what could be described as a bribe to overcome resistance can be contagious and consequently very expensive. Other practitioners who might have come on board without incentives could demand to be similarly compensated. It is rare for early years leaders to have access to incentives for overcoming resistance and facilitating agreement. Consequently, negotiation as a form of bargaining to gain agreement has little value for effecting change in early years provision and change leaders are advised instead to explore education and communication, facilitation and support, and participation and involvement as viable alternatives.

Manipulation and co-option may be employed in situations where other approaches are unlikely to work or are too expensive, in both time and money. Manipulation is a covert attempt to persuade or influence another through the selective use or filtering of information or the deliberate structuring of events. Manipulation entails shrewd, devious and potentially deceitful influence or control of others, alteration of information or any psychological attempt to mislead others for one's own advantage. Put simply, it is making people do what you want. Early years practitioners usually act swiftly to protect and defend any change that they think may compromise or violate professional principles or practice. Consequently, any attempt at manipulation diminishes the trustworthiness of those leading such changes, arouses strong emotions and intensifies practitioners' efforts to resist them. If those leading change in early years settings possess a hidden agenda and/or try to influence practitioners in underhand, surreptitious ways, they risk losing trust and respect, and consequently their power to persuade, direct, guide and lead practitioners.

> I'm never sure if we're being told the truth about what these changes mean . . . I'm sure we'll have to work harder, put in longer hours, but [the manager] says we just have to work smarter not harder. I've read the documentation . . . I don't understand it all . . . I do know it will mean that this job will be harder than it already is. It would be better if I thought she was being upfront about it.
>
> Childcare worker, pre-school centre

Authentic leadership in early years settings is grounded in trust, open communication, honesty and respect for the rights of others. Any leader who early years professionals believe to be manipulative, for example by telling 'white lies', playing mind games and scaring practitioners into accepting insupportable changes, soon loses their moral authority and legitimacy to lead.

The strategy of co-option is and has been used in early years provision to overcome opposition to and gain support for change from individuals, groups and organizations, for example by inviting a union or family representative to join a policy or management committee. On the surface, co-option can appear as a means of promoting participation and involvement. However, the underlying motivation is generally to secure endorsement for proposed changes. If co-optees discover that they have been lied to, tricked or manipulated into endorsing a change, they can respond very negatively, with greater resistance than previously encountered. In addition, if co-optees think that they are being manipulated, they may decide to influence a change in ways that are not in the best interests of early years provision. Given that other approaches to overcoming resistance are effective, manipulation and co-option offer early years leaders little benefit in addressing the current change directives.

Explicit and implicit coercion involves the use of authority or psychological force to overcome resistance to change. Coercion is a power strategy that relies on the use of authority, pressure or threat of sanction. Early years leaders who try to force practitioners to accept proposed change with threats of job or status loss, by blocking opportunities for promotion or, in extreme situations, by terminating their employment, tend to be regarded as inconsiderate, incompetent and unethical bullies.

> One adviser told us 'only those who embrace the changes will survive'. Did she mean that if I don't change, I'll lose my job? Can she do that?
>
> Pre-school educator, childcare centre

Proposed change that is coerced, forced or imposed, and unpopular, is rarely accepted by those affected by it.

> The problem is that there are important messages coming from the minister . . . changes that have to be made. I mean, we are simply told that we have to make these changes. But they might not fit our philosophy or pedagogy, yet we are still expected to do it. No one has asked me how I feel about what I've been told to do. Those people at the top need to find out how we feel about what they expect us to do.
>
> Early years teacher, children's centre

Coercion, be it implicit or explicit, ignites strong feelings of distrust, resentment and a desire to resist in many people. In early years provision, practitioners may accept coerced change in a crisis but it will never be popular. However, if immediate change is essential but unpopular, overcoming resistance by coercion may be a short-term option available to leaders. Unfortunately, leaders who adopt this tactic can experience considerable backlash from early years practitioners. Those leading change in early years settings should not consider this strategy unless other options for overcoming resistance are deemed inappropriate, inefficient or ineffective.

In addition to the major approaches above, two other techniques may be effective for early years leaders who wish to overcome practitioners' resistance to change. First, *advocacy* can persuade practitioners to accept proposed changes by presenting factual information, rational argument and appealing outcomes that encourage acceptance of proposed changes. This strategy can be combined with education and communication when need for change is not fully understood or considered important, when practitioners are not committed to change, or where change is perceived as complicated, large and risky. Advocacy involves presenting all sides of an issue and attempting to win over early years professionals by presenting available and relevant information in a reasoned argument that reaches logical conclusions.

Second, *problem resolution* as a technique to overcome resistance involves stating what appears to be the issue and then gathering facts, feelings and opinions to provide supporting information. Open communication and the participation and involvement of early years professionals can generate a number of alternative solutions that are then evaluated. Any differences of opinion can be resolved through critical discussion, with final decisions or solutions produced collaboratively by those concerned with and committed to quality improvement.

Those leading change in early years settings who encounter opposition and resistance to demands for change are advised to:

- identify the reasons behind practitioners' negativity and opposition;
- select the most appropriate approaches for channeling opposition into commitment.

However, those leading change in early years settings also need to be aware that they may adopt a subconsciously preferred approach to dealing with opposition and resistance, regardless of the individuals, issues and timeframe concerned. For example, some leaders acknowledge that their personal style is more 'people-oriented', making them more likely to default to facilitation and support or participation and involvement approaches, whereas others who are intellectually excited and challenged by change may focus more on educating and communicating with practitioners. Change leaders whose personal style focuses more on goal achievement and productivity (or when crisis demands immediate action) may default to the use of power, position and coercive strategies to push a particular change agenda forward. Change leaders who endorse the legitimacy of government directives and statutory mandates for early years provision may prefer to educate and negotiate with practitioners to gain their acceptance and commitment. Those who have become weary with and pessimistic about ongoing demands for change may default to more manipulative strategies to influence practitioners. Finally, when change leaders must ensure compliance with mandated change, they may find that listening to and validating the feelings and reactions of those who have to implement such changes will lessen resentment and resistance.

Successfully overcoming opposition and resistance usually requires the use of a combination of several strategies that reflect a pragmatic assessment of the situation and sensitive use of a range of tactics that capitalize on, but are not restricted to, personal strengths and preferences. Those leading change can positively influence early years practitioners during the process by the strategies they employ to conquer denial, insecurity, anger, worry, objections and opposition. Those change leaders who possess high levels of self-awareness are more likely to know and realistically evaluate their personal tendencies in such circumstances and adopt approaches and strategies that match and consequently eradicate the roots of opposition and resistance.

Encouraging proactive receptivity to change

Those who lead change effectively in early years provision acknowledge the legitimacy of practitioners' needs, concerns and interests and work sensitively with them to counteract any negativity and build stronger proactive receptivity to and readiness for change (Moyles 2006; Dunlop 2008).

Proactive attitudes towards change can be fostered in early years practitioners when change leaders encourage and expect regular and active participation in critical reflection; engagement with professional initiatives and political agendas; pursuit of lifelong learning; adoption of future-oriented and forward-thinking openness to unanticipated as well as expected challenges; and instigation and contribution to planning and implementing the processes of change.

To encourage proactive receptivity to change, informed early years leaders should:

- ensure that vision and mission statements are transparent and attractive;
- create and sustain supportive interpersonal relationships;
- communicate effectively, focusing on opportunities, benefits and ownership;
- remain calm, listening with understanding to practitioners' fears, concerns and emotions;
- identify 'change champions' from within settings and enlist their help;
- take an inclusive approach to involving and consulting with practitioners;
- empower practitioners through delegation, sharing and training;
- ensure emotional support and guidance is available and accessible;
- address practitioners' anxieties, concerns and stress;
- question, debate and evaluate the need and reasons for change, know what to change and what not to;
- assess the timing of change, know when to change and when not to;
- find, develop and provide the necessary resources ;
- address and eliminate excuses;
- use peer pressure to help bring on board non-rational objectors or obstructers;
- begin by instigating small-scale projects with a good probability of success and build on this success;
- draw on support from relevant networks, key contacts, partnerships and communities of practice;
- focus on finding solutions to obstacles by addressing ongoing questions, needs and concerns.

Early years professionals generally accept and commit to proposed changes in their own way, in their own time and in accordance with what they believe is in their best interests. The challenge for those leading change in early years settings is to create a workplace climate that makes the process of change attractive, easy and relevant for practitioners. Until those leading change address and eliminate sources of negativity, conflict and resistance, early years practitioners are unlikely to be ready or available to explore, commit to and implement change directives with optimism, anticipation and confidence.

Closing thoughts

There is a greater probability that change in early years provision will be accepted and supported when early years leaders and practitioners can see the 'big picture' and understand the reasons for and benefits of change, are meaningfully engaged with and confident about instigation, development and implementation processes, feel that their opinions, views and feelings are heard and taken into account, trust and have confidence in those leading change, have access to support, are given time to adjust, and are not expected to change too many things at once.

7

EFFECTING CHANGE THROUGH COLLECTIVE ENDEAVOUR

Coming together is beginning, keeping together is progress,
working together is success.
Henry Ford

Alone we can do so little; together we can do so much.
Helen Keller

This chapter explores:

▶ benefits of leading in partnership;
▶ identifying and nurturing change champions;
▶ harnessing the power of collaborative teams to effect change.

Leading change in early years provision is not easy or simple, and leaders rarely effect change by themselves. Successful implementation of sustainable change depends as much on stakeholders as it does on leaders. For change to be successfully implemented and embedded, those leading it must create a culture where change and its leadership are considered collective responsibilities and endeavours. Enlightened early years leaders seek to bring together a collaborative team of enthusiasts who willingly take responsibility for making change happen (Paige-Smith and Craft 2011). Such leaders appreciate the importance of identifying 'change champions', that is, those practitioners who, regardless of position, are receptive to, identify with and drive the vision for change forward through their positivity, commitment, motivation, initiative and empathy. They then become active advocates, sponsors, ambassadors and agents of change.

Most early years leaders appreciate and value collaborative teamwork and collective participation, especially when faced with pressure for change. They respect broad-based participation (McDowall Clark and Murray 2012) and understand that practitioners' leadership potential can be strengthened and refined through different opportunities and levels of responsibility for decision-making, action and accountability. Leaders who uphold the principle that leadership belongs to everyone (Siraj-Blatchford and Hallet 2013) also believe that everyone is in a position to make some contribution to the process (Ord et al. 2013). When addressing the current change directives, wise leaders communicate the benefits of and promote the concept of collective responsibility. The most effective way for early years leaders and practitioners to meet demands for change is to address it collectively by banding together and enabling everyone to become actively involved in meaningful ways.

> I believe in the power of everyone in the team, not just one person, to make change happen.
>
> Director, early years nursery

Because some early years practitioners can be suspicious of and cautious about change, nurturing interest in and empowering action for change though a culture of collective responsibility is an essential but challenging leadership activity. Unfortunately, the excitement, interest and energy of any leader can wither in the face of colleagues' apathy or negativity, and with that, the window of opportunity for making change happen can be lost. When those leading change invest in growing a culture of collective responsibility, they ensure that responsibility for making change happen is genuinely diffused among practitioners at all levels.

According to Grogan and Shakeshaft (2009), collective responsibility grows out of robust professional interpersonal relationships. In addition, Daws (2005) suggests that professional learning comes about through interpersonal relationships and dialogue with others that stimulate connections between ideas and context. Generating collective responsibility for leading change from and through interpersonal commitment to colleagues can be viewed as a form of collaborative learning because practitioners' broadened knowledge, skills and capability develop through learning with and from others. In early years settings, collaborative learning relationships can engage and grow capable practitioners who are committed to making change happen; and the more widely leadership is distributed throughout early years teams, the greater the potential for securing necessary change.

Benefits of collective leadership

Given the increasing complexity of early years provision and current pressures for reform and change, today's early years leaders encounter diverse and multiple demands on their time, energy, creativity and accountability. While many look to colleagues for assistance in meeting professional expectations, a collective approach to leadership may offer considerable benefit. Today, distributed leadership, that is, the formation of a genuine collaborative coalition where practitioners spontaneously and voluntarily enact leadership roles and functions to achieve common goals, is generally accepted as an appropriate and helpful way to meet various challenges faced by the sector, including directives for change.

Distributed leadership is a concept that is widely espoused but not necessarily well understood within the early years sector. The terminology currently used to denote the notion of collective responsibility for leadership includes reference to shared, devolved, decentralized, democratic, dispersed, collaborative and team leadership. The fundamental focus is on broad-based participation and joining together as equal partners. Distributed leadership in early years provision aims to encourage, enable and empower every practitioner to think, talk, act and assume some form of leadership responsibility. According to O'Gorman and Hand (2013), it is an effective use of practitioners' varied expertise. In addition, it becomes an inclusive opportunity because distribution necessitates the perforation, elimination or transcendence of hierarchical boundaries and levels. Insightful early years leaders appreciate that formal and arbitrary demarcation of roles and responsibilities can hinder receptivity to and readiness for change. Distributing leadership as a collective responsibility can help overcome this.

> I'm not a leader, I'm just a pre-school teacher, my focus is on the children . . . I know about what is best for children's learning, I'm not really interested in this talk about improving the system . . . and I wouldn't know where to start with it. As far as I'm concerned it's the director's job to do that.
>
> Teacher, nursery school

When leadership is embraced as a collective responsibility that transcends formal titles, positions and roles, early years practitioners are more likely to interact, learn with and from one another, and collaborate to construct shared meaning and understanding about proposed changes. Early years settings typically operate with a flattened hierarchy of power and authority, where practitioners share responsibility to some degree. However, when practitioners assume collective obligation for making change happen, more will spontaneously assume responsibility for engaging with and leading it.

Most early years professionals are familiar with and regularly employ the process of delegation to allocate duties appropriately. However, delegation is completely different from distributed or collective leadership. Delegation involves the intentional authorization of a practitioner to represent or act on behalf of the leader in relation to specified tasks or decisions. Power and responsibility are limited and the leader remains ultimately accountable. In contrast, leadership that is genuinely distributed and collective emerges from attitudes and approaches to practice (rather than being a function or technique) that focus on mobilizing leadership activity in every practitioner. It is not and cannot be allocated by a leader.

Rather, a culture of distributed leadership and collective responsibility for change in early years settings evolves from:

- belief and trust in the leadership potential of others and willingness of formal leaders to relinquish some power, authority and control;
- collaborative interpersonal relationships between practitioners;
- a mindset grounded in openness, freedom from arbitrary boundaries and recognition of value of the expertise of the many (as opposed to the few);
- dialogue and consultation;
- receptivity to new ideas, ways of working and change;
- professional values about collective responsibility and ownership.

> I continually ask myself . . . do I have the knowledge and skills to do what I'm being asked to do with these reforms? I often feel out of my depth . . . but I keep on going because I believe that if I model what to do, then some of the team will pick it up and run with it. Then it won't just feel like I am the only one responsible.
>
> Manager, early years learning centre

Early years leaders who willingly encourage collective responsibility for and open access to leadership opportunities within settings report that they feel less isolated and stressed by the pressures for change. However, other benefits flow out of collective responsibility for leading change, including:

- shared workload and responsibility;
- mutual and communal influence;
- better and more transparent decisions;
- more decision-making and action at grass-roots levels;
- greater collaboration and teamwork;
- enhanced practitioner interest and capability in leadership;
- growth in leadership capacity within the sector.

> Everyone's buying into the new framework right now, and that's great. But I wonder how their enthusiasm will be sustained. I think that if the team owns some of the action and responsibility, they'll be more interested in continuing with it over the longer term. You're more motivated if you own it.
>
> Team leader, early learning centre

Collective responsibility for leading change in early years settings is generated through:

- shared vision and purpose;
- consensual understanding of values and priorities;
- affirmation of practitioners' complementary and equally important roles;
- open communication, trust and confidentiality;
- ongoing discussion, debate and dialogue where everyone assumes responsibility for speaking and listening;
- respect for others' right to disagree;
- respectful and constructive approaches for resolving differences;
- recognition of the importance of mutual learning and improvement.

Early years leaders who foster collective responsibility for leading change tend to regard the parameters around leadership as fluctuating and permeable membranes that open spaces and opportunities for practitioners to access and engage in self-selected activity focused on proposed change, and encourage and support their efforts to do so. Moreover, experienced leaders appreciate that all leadership is transient and that they are responsible for growing leadership expertise within settings. As more practitioners demonstrate evolving competence and confidence in their capability for leading changes of different types and at varying levels, current leaders may wish to adapt, adjust, redefine and shift the parameters of their own roles and responsibilities within a broadening collective endeavour.

When leadership of change becomes a collective responsibility, different pathways open up for achieving desired outcomes; consequently, those leading change should focus on strategic plans and ends, rather than methods and means. Making change happen rarely comes about through a single plan or a simple solution. Sustainable change arises out of action that varies in novelty, scope and magnitude. Consequently, those leading change need to keep an open mind and remain flexible, tolerant and willing to learn as they relinquish control and encourage collective responsibility for leading change in early years settings.

Fostering collective commitment through change champions

Most early years settings are operated by relatively small teams of practitioners who understandably place more emphasis on delivering a quality day-to-day experience for young children than they do on initiating, implementing and sustaining change, even when it is mandated. However, early years leaders remain accountable for the delivery of high quality provision, and the recent government directives for reform make them responsible for stimulating practitioners' commitment to implementing changes in professional practice. Consequently, as well as building collective responsibility for effecting change, insightful leaders enlist the support of at least one enthusiastic practitioner to actively champion change alongside them.

Some early years leaders report that the current landscape of change has raised their personal levels of tension and stress. Perceptive early years leaders address such pressures by forming a coalition with appropriate allies (usually other practitioners) who display interest in the adoption, implementation and success of change. Such practitioners become 'champions of change' by working with the leader to increase others' receptivity to and readiness for change. Change champions display proactive attitudes and approaches to change and work to overcome potential negativity and resistance by encouraging commitment to change from everyone concerned.

In simple terms, those who champion change want improvement; they act using informal and formal means to persuade others to get on board. They 'walk the talk' and drive change forward through their enthusiasm and energy, encouraging others to actively engage, commit, take responsibility and assume ownership. Although they may not have formal authority to force through change themselves, enterprising change champions can make the difference between success and failure. Having the backing of at least one change champion is a practical strategy that helps early years leaders to increase commitment, overcome resistance, harness team resources, ensure successful implementation and increase the likelihood that change initiatives will become embedded as routine practice.

Generally, change champions are informal advocates who make a special effort to:

- engage the interest of those involved;
- build positive expectations about change;
- translate and regularly revitalize the vision for change;
- empathize with concerns, needs and interests of others;
- identify and address negativity and resistance;
- obtain commitment to both content and process of change;
- ensure better and new ways of working become evident in day-to-day routines;
- work to embed change initiatives in professional culture and practice.

Change champions who are effective advocates for change display certain qualities, skills and expertise:

- clear sense of purpose constructed from the reason behind and need for change, a vision of what can be achieved, ideas about a realistic timeframe, thoughts about appropriate strategies and an appreciation of process;
- capability and confidence to act based on respect for and from team members, strong interpersonal relationships, effective communication skills and political acumen;

- ability to draw on professional relationships, connections and networks to attract key players and team members, secure required resources, create a tipping point for change by persuading a sufficient number of resisters to become adopters;

- use of critical reflection to encourage a culture of learning that accepts and becomes informed by failure as well as success;

- knowledge and strategies for developing structures and systems to embed change into culture and practice.

When early years leaders form a working alliance with one or two change champions within settings, they capitalize on the knowledge, skills, expertise and relationships of practitioners who are enthusiastic about and committed to achieving a shared goal. This is the first step in building a critical number of practitioners who endorse proposed changes, implement action plans and ensure that change is embedded and secured within early years settings.

Rogers (2003) distinguishes various motivational orientations in relation to individual receptivity to and readiness for change. His categories and descriptors are useful guides for early years leaders who wish to identify those practitioners with the potential to act as change champions.

- **Innovators** – those who are visionary, adventurous, risk-taking, creative, come up with new ideas and ways of working, want to change the status quo (around 3 per cent).

- **Early adopters** – those who are perceived as being at the cutting edge of change, see the benefits and want change to succeed, whose opinion is respected, are prudent but willing to try out new ideas (around 13 per cent).

- **Early majority** – those who accept change but are more conservative, wary and thoughtful (around 34 per cent).

- **Late majority** – those who tend to be very conservative, uncomfortable with, sceptical and cautious about change, accept change only when solid evidence is available and endorsed by the majority (around 34 per cent).

- **Laggards** – those who are traditionalists, hold on to the old ways, resist and are slow to adjust to change (around 16 per cent).

Change champions tend to be found among those who are quick to adjust and commit to change, that is, the innovators and early adopters of change. Such early years practitioners drive change forward though their enthusiastic receptivity to change, willingness to participate in the process of change and pursuit of slow adjusters to embrace change. For them, the benefits outweigh any risks of change.

The commonly accepted 20/60/20 principle, when applied to receptivity to and readiness for change, can be a helpful guide for early years leaders who need to work with the range of reactions displayed by practitioners faced with reform directives. As a general rule, approximately 20 per cent of early years practitioners are excited and eager to embrace new ways of working and another 20 per cent fight against the new order, passively or actively, openly or covertly, rationally or irrationally, appropriately or inappropriately. The remainder, around 60 per cent, 'sit on the fence' or 'go with the flow', neither actively embracing nor actively resisting change proposals. They are similar to swinging voters who only commit to a choice once they perceive the personal benefits of a particular option.

The implications for those leading change are clear. While they are not solely responsible for motivating practitioners to embrace change, they are responsible for identifying early adopters and enthusiasts, and ensuring that those who want the change to succeed receive relevant and sufficient assistance, appropriate support and protection from resisters. Rather than wasting precious time and energy trying to overcome resistance, leaders' attention is better devoted to nurturing the energy and positivity of early adopters. Consequently, it is more productive to concentrate effort and time on those practitioners who display the greatest potential for effecting change. If and when early adopters' enthusiasm becomes contagious, it can influence those who are 'sitting on the fence' to come on board, and has potential to transform hardened resisters into adopters.

To be effective in enhancing receptivity to and readiness for change, change champions must be well informed about relevant aspects of proposed change, and how best to approach it. They create opportunities for dialogue about the vision for change to encourage others to commit. Capable change champions use interpersonal interactions to encourage early years practitioners to talk and work together, and keep them focused and motivated until sufficient momentum ensures that change is successfully implemented (Warrick 2009). Consequently, effective change champions in early years settings are those who command considerable respect from, and therefore can positively influence, other practitioners.

One other important consideration is the nature of the relationship and communication between leader and change champion. A change champion's activities should not be perceived or experienced as any threat to the formal leader's position and authority. Rather, an effective change champion does not supplant the leader but works with the formal leader as an ally and associate to build strong links between practitioners and those leading change, and between practitioners themselves. Consequently, communication between a change champion and leader needs to be open, honest, direct, two-way and regular.

Those who become effective change champions in and for early years provision clearly communicate:

- their investment in making a difference, that is, passionate belief that by doing things differently, a better future will be created for all;
- objectivity, flexibility and openness to new or more productive ideas, approaches and processes;

- vision and clarity regarding 'the big picture' and a new order for the future;
- courage to stand up, speak out and advocate for change while empathizing with others' anxieties and concerns;
- analytical ability to set priorities;
- collaborative interpersonal connections with other practitioners;
- willingness to share knowledge, skills and expertise with others;
- dedication to overcoming barriers and resistance;
- willingness to support, mentor and coach colleagues through the process of change;
- perseverance in implementing and embedding change initiatives.

Skilled change champions can help tip the balance of support towards change by working with a small number of early adopters and committed enthusiasts whose receptivity and positivity become infectious and spread to those early years practitioners who remain unconvinced or oppose change. Consequently, change champions can be crucial to the successful integration and sustainability of change into routine early years practice.

The power of collaborative teams in the change process

One of the most powerful resources that early years leaders can draw on when faced with pressure for complicated change is a strong collaborative team. The current reform agenda for early years provision demands that early years leaders and practitioners implement types and levels of change that can be challenging and difficult, in a work environment that offers little time and opportunity to think through, understand, plan for and effect change directives. In addition, the inherent complexity of the reform agenda requires some modification of early years practitioners' attitudes, thinking, behaviour, practice and professional identity. Consequently, successful implementation of the current reform agenda depends upon adjustment, accommodation and sometimes transformation of the way early years professionals think and act in relation to broad areas of practice.

Collaborative teamwork can be very powerful in helping early years practitioners to understand, come to terms with and commit to learning new ways of thinking and working, and is an important tool for those responsible for effecting change in early years provision (Stacey 2009). Teamwork is a people-oriented strategy for effecting and securing change, which is grounded in the belief that, for change to be successfully implemented, it is paramount to gain the cooperation and commitment of those who are involved. Teamwork is defined as a process of working collaboratively to achieve shared goals. It is a product of the cooperative and coordinated effort of a group of people working towards a common interest or concern (Sharp et al. 2012). In relation to change, teamwork becomes a process of involving people to commit to and invest in a new order. Change, therefore, is effected *with* a team, not imposed *on* a team.

Unfortunately, the pressure for change can heighten feelings of tension and stress within teams, which may give rise to more frequent challenging communications, tension between practitioners and a pervasive atmosphere of volatility. Instigating and securing change is rarely easy. Most teams experience some turbulence (highs and lows, ups and downs) during the process of change, indicators which should not be ignored by those leading change. Perceptive early years leaders are sensitive to warning signs that indicate turbulent rather than collaborative working relationships. The following indications can alert those leading change to potential problems with team functioning:

- practitioners talk more than listen;
- one or two practitioners dominate discussions and decision-making;
- some practitioners remain silent and do not contribute to discussion;
- the views and ideas of some practitioners are dismissed, ignored or criticized by more dominant team members;
- more frequent arguments (rather than constructively communicated differences of opinion);
- covert grumbling that may spawn obstructive behaviour by practitioners who are unhappy with decisions;
- little interest in cooperating to move towards general consensus;
- an absence of trust and helpfulness in the workplace.

When team members in early years settings remain negative about change, they make little effort to clarify roles, goals and specific tasks, to meet deadlines or to confront the difficulties and problems evident with a setting's interpersonal functioning. To address such issues, those leading change need to focus on generating enthusiasm, initiative and collective responsibility in every practitioner.

When early years teams function collaboratively, the work climate is supportive, freeing practitioners to experiment, take informed risks, say what they think, listen respectfully to one another, contribute in different and complementary ways, tolerate disagreement (because it is perceived as useful), and work through differences constructively. During times of change, those team members who participate in open discussion better understand what is expected and required, and generally cooperate willingly to meet the needs of the situation. Importantly, they learn from experience and each other, using reflective discussion to review and improve practice and processes as well as their collective successes and failures. Collaborative teamwork in early years settings opens up opportunities for those leading change to distribute, delegate and extend collective leadership responsibilities to practitioners on the basis of expertise, interest or circumstance.

Early years leaders who work in partnership with teams increase the likelihood that change will be effected because:

- they draw on the diverse talents of team members and integrate specialized perspectives, knowledge, skills and expertise to improve the quality of the outcomes; and

- working cooperatively helps build and sustain the enthusiasm, engagement and energy required to bring about complex outcomes.

Because collaborative teamwork can capitalize on the different strengths, skills and judgement that team members bring to the change endeavour, teams can achieve more than one individual is able to. Collaborative teamwork also helps to distribute ownership of and responsibility for leading change by encouraging practitioners to access and undertake a wider range of roles and tasks.

> The new laws and regulations have set our service the biggest challenge we've experienced, . . . most of the team are finding it extremely challenging to upgrade our training and skills, . . . to take on a broader range of duties.
>
> Team leader, children's centre

It is widely acknowledged that banding together in teams offers numerous benefits for early years provision (Aubrey 2011). When faced with the current reform agenda, early years practitioners who work collaboratively are more likely to focus on the positives, counteract the negatives and adjust faster to new circumstances. Because of its essentially encouraging focus, collaborative teamwork can boost creativity and innovation, improve morale and job satisfaction, foster the emergence of support networks, open access to a broader skill set and promote quality improvement. Other benefits arising out of collaborative teamwork include:

- improved confidence, motivation and personal satisfaction;
- greater clarity in thinking and ideas from dialogue, discussion and reflection;
- wider range of ideas, options and possibilities than could be generated by one individual in isolation;
- greater practitioner engagement in strategic thinking and action;
- fuller appreciation of each team member's contribution;
- greater understanding of and empathy with each other's needs and concerns;
- more efficient and effective use of resources, especially time;
- opportunities for meaningful learning with and from colleagues;
- greater sense of ownership of and collective responsibility for successes and achievements.

> Working together to solve problems and knowing that my input has been heard makes me feel better about myself and what I can do with the new framework, . . . it feels more inclusive, . . . having ownership is a good feeling.
> Early years educator, pre-school centre

Regrettably, many early years settings continue to experience high staff turnover (Aubrey 2011). Retention is a serious issue, especially when early years professionals are required to address complicated changes for reform. The instability caused by staff turnover is a perennial and structural issue for the early years sector and hampers any setting's potential to respond effectively to demands for change (Puffett 2013). While loss of expertise that has been built up over time is sufficiently problematic, the fact that collaborative teamwork continues to be restricted by the need to focus on team-building keeps it at a less operationally efficient stage of team development (Rodd 2013a).

Early years leaders who wish to harness and draw on the power of collaborative teamwork to effect change:

- know the strengths, abilities, interests and vulnerabilities of practitioners;
- match the talents and resources of team members to goals, purposes and tasks;
- communicate clear expectations regarding the necessity and benefits of collaborative activity;
- nurture a culture of learning by offering team members varied opportunities to develop requisite knowledge and skills;
- support the activity and efforts of teams and practitioners through mentoring and coaching;
- allow time for team members to learn new skills and adjust.

The development of collective responsibility for making change happen in early years provision is encouraged by leaders and change champions who:

- articulate a vision that inspires, engages and briefs others about direction, general processes and estimated timeframe for any proposed change;
- communicate openly and empathically about the challenges and opportunities presented by change proposals;
- identify early adopters, encouraging them to talk openly about how much they value the change, how it will be better for all concerned and what they hope to see happen;
- involve team members in designing the *how* of change, that is, the strategies and processes that will enable change initiatives to be implemented and sustained;

- are highly visible and accessible throughout the process of change;
- encourage collaborative learning opportunities for others to acquire essential knowledge and skills to meet new circumstances and ways of working;
- ensure that progress is monitored and reviewed regularly;
- highlight small successes throughout the process of change, encouraging personal narratives that focus on individual contributions to and overall benefits of change.

Closing thoughts

Insightful early years leaders appreciate that they cannot take sole responsibility for making change happen. The establishment of genuine, working coalitions, collaborations and partnerships underpins the successful implementation of the directives specified in current reform agendas. Those leading such change in early years settings benefit from considerable input from practitioners who work competently in collaborative teams as well as individually. Early years leaders who understand the advantages of banding together, working collaboratively and in partnership with those concerned with proposed change focus on enhancing practitioners' willingness to participate and assume collective responsibility. Sustainable change is more easily achieved where opportunity for leadership is genuinely distributed, change champions and early adopters are identified, and collaborative teamwork is encouraged and rewarded.

8

SUSTAINING CHANGE IN A CULTURE OF LEARNING

The future belongs to those who prepare for it.
Ralph Waldo Emerson

This chapter explores:

▶ the role of learning in effecting change;
▶ learning in technical and adaptive change;
▶ learning organizations and culture;
▶ the relationship between learning, leadership and change;
▶ the impact of learning on developing leadership capacity.

The key to helping the early years sector meet the challenges of today's complex agenda for quality improvement is to increase early years professionals' receptivity to, readiness for, enthusiasm about and commitment to change by building a culture of learning that every practitioner willingly subscribes to. Such a culture helps develop a range of thinking skills and consequently empowers practitioners to instigate and address change. Early years settings that manifest a culture of learning are ' . . . open, transparent, accountable, inclusive and adaptable . . . and safeguard diversity, knowledge and experimentation' (Painter 2014: 41).

Sustained professional learning in the early years workforce underpins professional growth and transformation, which in turn ensures that provision for young children and families remains current and relevant (Ord et al. 2013). Any change initiative is more likely to succeed if those concerned believe that they possess or can acquire adequate understanding, knowledge, skills and confidence to meet the demands of working differently. Where early years professionals lack necessary expertise, access to varied opportunities for developing requisite ability and proficiency is essential, and produces enhanced capability as well as other gains in professional knowledge and understanding. In many ways, the courage, vigour and stamina that are required to drive change forward originate in continuous professional learning.

Most proposals, frameworks and agendas for change necessitate considerable shifts in early years professionals' thinking and practice. Hydon and I'Anson (2009) encourage Australian early years professionals to think about their approach to the recent Early Years Learning Framework by prefacing their suggestions with William Van Horne's pertinent quote:

Nothing is too small to learn and nothing is too big to attempt.

Hydon and I'Anson echo the beliefs of other authors (for example, Lochrie 2009; Urban et al. 2011; Nutbrown 2012) who believe that, to survive and succeed in these times of intense change, early years settings must be staffed by a well-qualified workforce and, to enhance quality, all early years professionals must refine familiar practice and learn new ways of working with young children and families. Nutbrown (2012: 21) states that learning by the early years workforce needs to be lifelong, emphasizing that the 'qualifications journey should not end with the first qualification'.

Learning new ways is based on early years professionals' willingness and confidence to move out of their familiar comfort zone into a new and perhaps unaccustomed learning zone. The viability and sustainability of relevant early years provision will be achieved only when every practitioner accepts responsibility for engaging in ongoing learning. Indeed, only those early years professionals who become curious and dedicated lifelong learners who know how to learn and think will increase their receptivity, responsivity and readiness to address the current directives and proposals for enhanced quality. Urban et al. (2011) suggest that professional growth through improved reflective practice by early years professionals may be strengthened by the creation of critical learning communities.

When individuals choose to engage with learning as an important part of their identity and life, they grow and enhance their personal well-being and sense of fulfilment (that is, Maslow's concept of self-actualization). In addition, they either possess or acquire three important attributes that distinguish those who are competent leaders, lifelong learners and thinkers, and therefore capable of leading change:

- flexibility (openness to possibility);
- adaptability (ability to adjust to changed context or circumstances);
- resilience (buoyancy or ability to recover from difficulties).

Ongoing engagement with learning and thinking whets an appetite for the achievement of greater understanding and creativity in personal and professional endeavours. For early childhood professionals, it can stimulate the reinvigoration, re-energization and regeneration of those who have suffered burnout or rust-out as a result of endemic and challenging change.

Encouraging the adoption of lifelong learning and thinking as an integral part of every early years practitioner's professional identity and responsibility is a means of building a well-qualified, multi-skilled, adaptable, empowered and resilient workforce.

Identification with the need for and benefits of lifelong learning will only come about when a culture of learning is encouraged and supported in early years provision, networks and communities that offer genuine and varied opportunities for participation in professional learning and development. Learning in adults, especially by early childhood professionals faced with the pressure for change, is enhanced when it is contextualized within an overall strategy, aligned with current objectives, and is meaningful, coherent and relevant for each learner. A culture of learning and thinking grows out of workplace values, structure, climate and action that respect, validate and respond to the diverse and changing needs of learners. The broad objective of a culture of learning is the development of capability and initiative through collaborative knowledge- and skill-building in an atmosphere of trust and respect.

The role of learning in change

Typically, modern organizations, including early years settings, encounter two major categories of change: technical or adaptive (Heifetz 1994). These two different categories call for different responses from people and systems, and consequently demand different approaches to leadership.

Technical change is more straightforward: it calls for the organization and system to respond in ways that are relatively familiar, routine and already present in its repertoire of skills and processes (Aigner 2011). Those who successfully lead technical change ensure that it is deconstructed into smaller, functional tasks with achievable outcomes and timescales. The majority of change in any organization, including early years provision, is technical, that is, change involving small adjustments to day-to-day routine tasks, thereby ensuring that settings run smoothly, reliably and efficiently. Problems and solutions are easily identified and applied. To begin to address the current reform agenda, Hydon and I'Anson (2009) recommend that early years professionals first look at their practice and decide what could be improved. Any improvement to early years practice, regardless of scope or size, is an example of technical change.

Technical change is sometimes referred to as bureaucratic change because it ensures the stability and continuity of the system. Other examples of such changes in early years settings are modifying mealtimes and menus, varying observation, recording and assessment formats, and adjusting learning experience and activity types and schedules. Maintaining the status quo, keeping the system on track, ensures survival until new challenges expose the fact that the old system no longer works well and doesn't meet the demands of the present circumstances. Ultimately, if early years professionals and settings are not flexible and do not adapt, they do not survive.

On the other hand, adaptive change calls for people and systems to learn, adapt to new circumstances and find new possibilities, especially where improvement is the goal. This can be referred to as innovative or transformational change because the existing responses in the system's repertoire have become inadequate or fail to meet the demands of the scope, degree and pace of the challenge. Solutions appropriate for more difficult and complex adaptive change are found only through horizon-scanning (Sharp et al. 2012), experimentation, creative problem-solving, risk-taking and finding novel or unusual strategies.

Responding to pressure for adaptive change for improvement also requires that early years professionals and settings learn. Sharp et al. (2012: 36–7) suggest that, when those leading change are guided by a vision that incorporates and responds to multiple perspectives from a collaborative and solutions-focused approach, they can secure better outcomes for young children and families. Leading adaptive change therefore depends upon keeping informed of the latest information about and developments in policies and practice. Examples of adaptive change in early years provision are the implementation of new quality standards and new learning and curriculum frameworks, addressing long-term family dissatisfaction, addressing poor staff retention rates and low levels of staff motivation, the development of integrated, multi-disciplinary provision and resolving antipathy and strain expressed by stakeholders that arise from diverse values, backgrounds, assumptions, expectations and needs.

The need for adaptive change can be more difficult to understand, identify and accept because it can generate uncertainty and anxiety about possible pathways forward. Consequently, solutions may not be easy to find, and suggestions may be challenged, resisted or obstructed. Complicated change, such as the current challenges experienced in the early years sector, is often unfamiliar, unpredictable, evolving and dependent on people who are both part of the problem and the solution to the problem (Kahane 2004). Meeting pressure for complex change demands that people work together collaboratively in order to make the whole system function better (Sharp et al. 2012). Responding appropriately to pressure for complex change in the early years sector requires practitioners and settings to commit to building a culture of learning and thinking (Stonehouse and Gonzales-Mena 2004) where knowledge, experience and expertise are grown and shared with the many as opposed to being reserved for the few. Early years provision will be better equipped to meet pressure for adaptive change if a strong culture of learning and thinking is in place.

Early years settings as learning organizations

Early years settings that have incorporated a culture of sustained learning and thinking into professional identity and practice have systems, mechanisms and processes in place for building capability and capacity within their workforce. This philosophy embodies a set of attitudes, values and practices that encourage and enable continuous learning of every member in the workplace. Such early years settings facilitate the learning of staff in all positions by expecting, guiding and supporting the modification, adaptation and transformation of practice according to changes in external circumstances and contexts. As such, these early years settings display many characteristics of Senge's 'learning organization' (Senge 2006; Taylor and Senge 2014) including:

- workplace climates that value trust, open communication and people, and encourage learning and innovation at all levels;
- infrastructure and processes that encourage interaction across boundaries, for example networking, mentoring and coaching;
- strategies, techniques and tools that encourage team and individual learning, for example flexible thinking skills and creative problem-solving;
- interest in, motivation, commitment and ability to learn and adapt.

Such settings establish a professional culture that works for, not against, improvement, reform and change and foster a mindset in early years workplaces that values and facilitates collaborative and lifelong learning, flexible and creative thinking, continuous improvement and constructive innovation.

Early years settings that function as learning organizations are future-oriented, interested in shaping the form and direction of provision, value diversity, encourage full and active participation of everyone concerned, respect and validate individual and team efforts to learn, think and improve, make time to enable everyone to reflect and rethink, and tolerate mistakes and failure – provided lessons are learned. Only those early years settings with a genuine culture of learning and thinking integrated into professional practice have the real ability to respond to increasingly dynamic, unpredictable and changing political and social pressures.

> The foundation stage teacher talked to us as a team about the need to improve our observation and planning. She asked us to come up with ideas about how we wanted to go about this . . . did we want formal input from her, did we want someone outside – an expert – to come in, did some of us want to go on a course, would anyone in the team do some research and contribute in a staff meeting? It was great having a choice of options, I felt that we had some control [over] how we could learn new ways . . . not just given a photocopy and told to read it sometime.
>
> Teacher, primary school

Empowering learning and thinking within early years teams is very important in the development of a learning culture. When early years practitioners make decisions, control the processes and take ownership of their own learning and thinking, they broaden their understanding about the role, outcome and relationship of learning to their setting's structures and procedures, and consequently about its success in meeting demands for change.

Senge (2006) identifies five key factors that underpin the creation of a genuine learning organization:

- personal mastery where individuals learn because they want to, are free to pursue personal goals and their learning is valued and validated;
- cognitive models where individuals' internal understanding of organizational development and functioning shapes their actions and decisions;
- shared vision where commitment is enhanced through the alignment of personal vision with that of the organization;
- team learning where collaborative learning is valued, expected and supported in recognition of the synergy generated by collective (as opposed to individual) ability and functioning;
- systems thinking where access to the 'big picture' and appreciation of how one change can affect other people, processes and structures help encourage learning and thinking.

Such a culture of learning evolves within early years settings when early years professionals understand *how* to learn, are willing to share knowledge, experience and expertise with others, and are willing to do things differently because of growing confidence and ability with a range of flexible thinking skills that are applied to the acquisition of new knowledge, understanding and capabilities.

> I hope that one of the outcomes of our team having to respond to the documentation is that they become inspired to aspire, they want to learn because they want to improve . . . and because essentially we are a community of learners, adults and children together.
>
> Manager, childcare centre

A culture of learning and thinking helps early years professionals meet demands for complex adaptive change because it supports and encourages:

- anticipation of change as a normal part of contemporary life and work;
- greater initiative, responsiveness, flexibility, adaptability and resilience to external circumstances and environments;
- interest in and proficiency to meet new challenges;
- team as well as individual learning and development;
- the use of learning outcomes to achieve better results and growth.

One of the major challenges for those leading change in today's early years provision is to ensure that their setting has processes in place that stimulate and engage every practitioner, including themselves, with continuous learning, thinking, improvement and capability development as an integral part of their professional responsibility and practice. A positive attitude to learning is usually associated with increased self-esteem and confidence as well as a positive attitude to change (Claxton 2002). However, those leading change must do more than simply endorse ongoing learning; they must ensure that learning is placed at the centre of leadership practice. Authentic leaders of change regard learning and thinking as core priorities and act to generate a workplace climate in which learning is at the top of everyone's personal agenda. They act as role models by engaging in and being enthusiastic about learning and thinking, and are perceived by others as active learners.

Factors that hamper the development of a culture that is conducive to learning and thinking include:

- hoarding information, knowledge, experience and expertise;
- competition rather than cooperation between employees;
- ineffective teamwork;
- hidden personal agendas rather than shared vision;
- interest in exclusive personal benefit rather than inclusive shared benefit;
- lack of senior administrative interest and investment, especially time;
- micromanagement and top-down, autocratic leadership styles.

In early years settings, a culture of learning and thinking evolves from early years professionals' values and positive attitudes towards developing, learning and improving together to better meet the expectations and needs of the young children, families and local communities they work with and for.

> I know some of the educators feel nervous about participating in the professional development programme but I talk to them about aspiring for their own development, helping them understand that it's a pathway that will make a difference in their life . . . that it can be exciting to have new experiences, be exposed to different ideas, to feel free to ask questions and to learn new skills.
> Director, children's centre

Although training programmes do contribute to the development of a learning organization, training alone does not create a genuine culture of learning and thinking. In fact, it is estimated that only about 10 per cent of workplace learning occurs through formal training, 20 per cent comes through communicating with and feedback from others, and the remaining 70 per cent comes from practical experiences, tasks and problem-solving, that is, from hands-on, on-the-job participation (Lombardo and Elchinger 1996). Training generally is associated with the acquisition of specific skills and outcomes, whereas the focus of a learning organization is towards the development of higher-order thinking, knowledge, attitudes and understanding. Farrago and Skyrme (1995) propose that, for individuals and teams, four different types of learning underpin the creation of a true learning organization:

- **Level 1** – learning facts, knowledge, processes and procedures.
- **Level 2** – learning new job skills that are transferable to other situations and contexts.
- **Level 3** – learning to adapt.
- **Level 4** – learning to learn.

In relation to change, Level 1 learning is appropriate only for minor or technical changes, for example fine-tuning or small modifications to existing policies and practice. Level 2 learning is required when existing practice is inadequate for new circumstances and new knowledge or skills must be acquired, for example new approaches to literacy or numeracy. Level 3 learning is required for changes to systems and process or for issues and problems that demand new solutions, for example implementing new quality standards or a curriculum framework. Level 4 learning is required for unforeseeable situations and circumstances where basic assumptions are challenged, experience is rethought, existing knowledge is re-framed, creativity and innovation are critical, and future-oriented solutions are vital – for example, implementing an agenda for reform. Adaptive change demands higher-level understanding, knowledge and competencies by those leading and affected by such change and consequently requires Levels 2, 3 and 4 learning ability.

Although formal training and on-the-job experience will always be necessary, *learning to learn* has become the critical ability for surviving in modern society because it enables people to acquire the skills needed to deal with and adapt to changes in the environment. Given that much of the knowledge and skills acquired during education and pre-service training soon becomes redundant, and the context for early years provision continually changes, it is essential that early years professionals are equipped with tools that they can apply to new situations requiring learning, thinking, adaptation and possible transformation.

> When I run a staff development session, I talk with each team about what they're doing, why they are doing it, where it can be improved, how this fits with the setting and sector, and how they can have an impact on improving their work with children and families. I want them to understand why they are doing this.
>
> Early years training consultant

The current reform agendas are asking most early years professionals to respond to changes that were not envisaged during their training or current work experience. To successfully meet these demands, early years practitioners need to be capable of learning and thinking in ways and about circumstances that cannot be predicted, to become future-oriented and extend their awareness forward to meet unimaginable challenges. Early years professionals who understand *how* to learn possess the requisite confidence to show initiative, capitalize on unexpected opportunities, assume responsibility and consequently make positive contributions to the quality of early years provision. Learning to learn, that is, the acquisition of a set of skills that enable learners to learn more effectively and become lifelong learners (Greany and Rodd 2003), is the most effective tool for empowering and maximizing professional capacity in the early years sector and an area that those leading change in early years settings need to be familiar with.

> I challenge myself to learn something new every week because I want to make a difference for the children in this childcare centre.
>
> Early years teacher, children's centre

Early years settings can be transformed into learning organizations when leaders create a safe, supportive workplace environment where individual differences in approaches to learning, thinking, acting and achieving results are respected, sharing and collaboration are expected, input and risk-taking are encouraged, and personal as well as professional development is supported.

Building a culture of learning and thinking

In order to transform early years settings into learning organizations that foster a culture of learning and thinking, competent early years leaders incorporate lifelong learning as part of the shared vision and mutually agreed long-term goals and strategies. Because its main aim is people empowerment, it is essential that every early years practitioner commits to lifelong learning as part of ongoing personal and professional development. The establishment and maintenance of a culture of learning and concomitant thinking within early years settings is a long-term initiative that requires serious involvement, investment and dedication.

> I am passionate about doing a good job and I love being part of a good team, so I put energy into improving my own work and helping others do their work better too.
>
> Director, pre-school centre

A culture of reciprocal learning and thinking can make a significant impact on quality improvement in early years provision when it:

- kindles high expectations about responsibility for personal learning and personal growth in practitioners at every level;
- is anchored in trust, open communication and positive relationships;
- advocates co-learning, collective enquiry, mutual enrichment and distributed leadership;
- encourages sharing, cooperation and teamwork;
- is needs-based, data-driven and result-focused;
- is linked to vision, mission and strategic goals;
- values and stimulates experimentation, informed risk-taking, courageous decision-making, creativity and innovation;
- underpins professional dialogue and development activity in all staff;
- is open to scrutiny and accountability for quality improvement and performance.

Early years leaders have many and varied responsibilities but they must not neglect their role in encouraging and enabling learning, thinking, reflection and the acquisition of the skills of learning in practitioners. Authentic early years leaders can transform settings into learning organizations with a culture of sustained learning and attendant thinking when they:

- act as 'lead learners', ensuring that their own engagement in and enjoyment of learning and thinking is visible;
- look for, uncover and help practitioners to identify their own potential, goals and options for development;
- listen to practitioners and involve them in identifying relevant learning opportunities;
- communicate clearly regarding direction, plans, targets and requisite knowledge, skills, experience and expertise;
- present identified learning and development needs as positive opportunities rather than deficiencies or problems to be rectified;
- expect, encourage and validate collaborative co-learning and teamwork;
- plan for a range of learning styles, recognizing that practitioners learn in different ways and at different rates;
- overcome or minimize barriers such as time, funding and deadlines;
- offer access to varied and challenging work roles and responsibilities;
- offer access to a range of professional development opportunities including informal training, external courses, shadowing, mentoring and coaching;
- promote learning by communicating, highlighting and personifying its benefits for individuals, teams, settings, children and families.

Such strategies can help create a workplace climate where everyone teaches, everyone thinks, everyone learns, everyone grows and the quality of early years provision improves. Practitioners' motivation grows because, when new skills are acquired, confidence, capability, productivity and employability are enhanced.

> I deliberately choose different professional development experiences so that I broaden the range of work activities that I'm exposed to. I want to learn how to work at a higher level, how to make a real difference and how to move the early years sector forward.
>
> Manager, local authority child and family services

Those leading change in early years settings who wish to promote the development of a culture of learning and thinking are encouraged to reflect upon the following issues and questions.

- **Learning focus** – do they have sufficient understanding of each practitioner's strengths, deficiencies and needs to accurately target and match learning and improvement needs and activities?

- **Professional development** – what opportunities and conditions are most likely to motivate and support each early years practitioner's learning and improvement needs, as well as enhance quality and leading practice?

- **Context** – in what ways could the early years workforce and local communities contribute to identified learning and improvement needs, for example, are any existing learning networks, communities, mentors and coaches appropriate and available?

- **Action** – what strategies are likely to have the greatest impact on learning and improvement during times of change? What impediments and obstacles exist, and how might they be overcome?

- **Sustainability** – how can the energy and effort put into learning and improvement by practitioners be recognized, validated, reinforced and rewarded?

Early years leaders and practitioners who understand how to learn and value lifelong learning foster a professional workplace culture that prioritizes growth and improvement. Consequently, they have acquired the confidence to approach change with a 'can do' attitude when it is identified, presented or demanded. They display a 'development mindset' and tend to be intrinsically motivated to stretch themselves, to learn, improve and contribute their best efforts. Because learning is integrated into daily life and work, they are less likely to resist pressure for change and are more likely to embrace it for the opportunities and benefits it can offer.

Learning, leadership and change

Leadership and learning are indispensable to each other.
John Fitzgerald Kennedy

President J.F. Kennedy clearly understood and articulated the link between learning and leadership in a speech prepared for delivery on the day of his assassination in 1963. Since then, many authors have connected leadership with learning, for example Fullan (2001), Harris and Lambert (2003), Senge (2006), Kouzes and Posner (2012) and Siraj-Blatchford and Hallet (2013). They argue that learning and leadership are inextricably intertwined, with leaders holding particular responsibility for stimulating collective learning in colleagues. Competent leadership is viewed as a catalyst for collaborative learning because it inspires enquiry, stimulates dialogue and debate, advocates reflection, encourages creative and innovative thinking, supports the construction of meaning, and subsequently the development of better practice.

According to Fullan (2001: 10) ' . . . good leaders foster good learning at other levels'. In early years provision, authentic leadership creates opportunities for practitioners to learn and think, and to learn together. It produces practitioners who know how to learn, and who use learning and knowledge to think about, create and respond to demands for change within settings. Competent authentic leadership both pushes and pulls practitioners into a zone of learning.

Capable leadership in early years settings encourages practitioners' willingness and capacity to embrace a culture of learning and thinking, and by so doing, to function as curious learners and critical thinkers within a collective learning community. A visible culture of learning and thinking in early years settings is evidenced through displays of trust, genuineness, respectful interpersonal relationships and effective pedagogy. Such settings are more likely to be responsive to pressure for improvement and therefore more amenable to change.

Constructive improvement arises from change leaders' expectations about and support for individual and collective learning, as well as early years practitioners' commitment to advancing quality through examining and modifying knowledge and practice (Wong et al. 2012). Change in early years settings can be a product of specific interconnected ideas that early years professionals use to guide and strengthen collaboration, improve practice and thereby contribute to improvement (Wong et al. 2012). These ideas cover flexibility about rules, risk-taking, collaborating, sharing knowledge and learning from practice. When early years practitioners face pressure for quality improvement, coming together as a discerning learning community can encourage professional conversations focused on identifying and challenging outdated ways of working and finding new possibilities.

Just as learning and leadership are intertwined and occur simultaneously, learning and change are inextricably interwoven and synchronous.

Carl Rogers (1967) highlighted the interrelationship between learning and change in the following passage (Russell 2002: 26).

> *We are, in my view, faced with an entirely new situation in education where the goal of education, if we are to survive, is the facilitation of change and learning. The only man who is educated is the man who has learned how to learn; the man who has learned how to adapt and change; the man who has realized that no knowledge is secure, that only the process of seeking knowledge gives the basis for security. Changingness, a reliance on process rather than upon static knowledge, is the only thing that makes any sense as a goal for education in the modern world.*

Rogers's ideas challenge professionals concerned with education, including those leading early years provision, to promote a culture of learning in which practitioners feel encouraged, enabled and empowered to learn, become better at what they do and in doing so contribute to constructive change.

In early years provision, the amalgamation of learning, leadership and change lays the foundation for the development of a professional learning community that focuses everyone's attention and energy on change for improvement, and becomes the keystone for developing leadership capacity and nurturing more potential leaders.

Learning and the development of capacity for change leadership

Efforts to initiate and implement the complicated directives for change demanded by current reform agendas for early years provision are unlikely to be successful if change leadership is dependent on one or two people. Change in early years settings is more likely to be achieved when practitioners acquire and demonstrate broad-based aspiration and capability for contributing to the functions and responsibilities of leadership. Building a culture of learning and thinking is a prudent investment for creating a pool of leaders within early years settings who are capable and ready to assume leadership roles and responsibilities if and when the need arises.

> Undertaking EYPS [Early Years Professional Status accredited qualification] has given me the opportunity to look at my strengths and weaknesses, identify areas where I can improve, . . . it gave me direction for where I need to grow and develop as a leader, so my work is better now . . . and I am prepared for the next stage of my professional career.
>
> Manager, childcare centre

Lack of leadership capacity is identified as a major stumbling block to the expansion of a skilled early years workforce in many countries

(Urban et al. 2011; Sharp et al. 2012; Ord et al. 2013; Campbell-Evans et al. 2014). Wise early years leaders appreciate that all leadership is transient and that disruption to and unexpected changes in leadership can be very stressful and detrimental to the stability, continuity and quality of provision for young children and families. Therefore, it is important that policies and plans for leadership development and succession within a setting are in place, and that early years leaders appreciate their role in identifying, recruiting and cultivating leadership aspiration and potential in others.

Most early years leaders readily acknowledge that considerable leadership potential remains untapped in many practitioners. Ord et al. (2013: 15) outline an innovative and refreshing approach to developing pedagogical leadership in early childhood education in New Zealand, which has much to offer those leading change in early years provision elsewhere. They describe findings from a Maori immersion early childhood centre based research study, Te Kopae Piripono (2006), concerning four identified types of collective and distributed leadership accountability that are integral aspects of Maori community-based leadership in early education provision:

- having responsibility (designated roles and positions of responsibility);
- being responsible (an individual's attitude and actions related to being professional, acting ethically and appropriately, being honest, being positive, and being open to others and different perspectives);
- taking responsibility (courage, risk-taking, having a go, taking up the challenge and trying new things);
- sharing responsibility (sharing power, roles and positions through relationships, interaction and engagement with others, being able to listen to others' points of view, acknowledging different perspectives, and asking for and providing assistance).

These four distinct types of responsibility and accountability reveal how it can be possible for everyone to be empowered to enact some form of leadership during change, thereby growing leadership capacity from within early years provision.

When leading change is conceived as incorporating 'having, being, taking and sharing', it opens up possibilities and opportunities for every early years practitioner to assume a role that resonates with and is appropriate for individual expertise, interest and context. For example, some early years practitioners will *have* designated responsibility for change through their position of teacher or coordinator; others can *be* responsible for leading change through their receptive attitudes and positive actions. Some early years practitioners will *take* responsibility for leading change by voluntarily stepping up and trying different ways of working. Finally, those early years practitioners who have taken some responsibility for leading any form of change within a setting can *share* this with others by making space, opening opportunities and encouraging engagement. These ideas are particularly pertinent for those leading change in today's early years settings because they highlight the fact that leadership can be genuinely distributed where the prevailing culture in the workplace is one of collaboration, commitment and community.

The process of distributed leadership is a key strategy for addressing the important issues of capacity and succession because it is a way of growing leaders from within the setting. Fullan (2001) argues that a learning-focused culture allows and encourages leadership to be exercised at all levels. Early years leaders who wish to identify, assess and develop leadership potential from within settings need to open up space for practitioners to take up leadership opportunities. They must be willing to relinquish some power and authority and ensure that the parameters of leadership function and responsibility are flexible and permeable. Early years settings with a culture of learning for continuous improvement can build leadership talent and expand leadership capacity from within through the development of practitioners, thereby ensuring continued growth in practitioners' capabilities, leadership capacity and quality. Interestingly, Fullan (2001) emphasizes that leadership which is distributed through all levels can produce a supply of future leaders for the system (that is, the early years sector) as a whole. In his view, leadership is and can be reconceptualized as building capacity. In times of limited training budgets, it is important to capitalize on every opportunity to build leadership capacity from and within early years provision.

Distributed leadership has the potential to counteract some of the factors that contribute to increased stress and high turnover of experienced practitioners. Fenech's findings (2006) reveal that increasing regulation and statutory requirements, higher expectations regarding quality improvement and accountability, perceived lack of recognition and trust as autonomous professionals, limited opportunities for individual professional development and training needs, and restricted promotional opportunities and career pathways can generate significant job dissatisfaction, frustration, discontent and lack of fulfilment for some early years professionals. Opportunity to take the lead with various change initiatives may not only contribute to capacity-building, but also help to retain experienced practitioners by ameliorating such professional disaffection.

Leadership capacity in the early years sector includes understanding about the principles and practice of leadership, contextualized knowledge and expertise, emotional intelligence, critical thinking, ability to make connections, future and improvement orientations, and political and business acumen (adapted from Stoll et al. 2002). Harris and Lambert (2003) propose that increased leadership capacity in educational organizations, which included early years settings, evolves from:

- acknowledgement that leadership is a shared endeavour;
- recognition that every team member has the potential and right to function as a leader;
- rejecting dependence on a single authority figure;

- values and a culture of distributed power and authority;
- commitment to learning that leads to constructive change.

In times of complex change, it is important that potential early years leaders are equipped with the knowledge, skills and expertise required for flexible leadership through a learning culture that includes distributed leadership as a key professional development strategy alongside formal training, on-the-job opportunities, mentoring and coaching. However, given the pressing need for more effective leaders of change, three important questions still need to be answered.

- What qualifications, training and on-the-job experiences best prepare early years practitioners to assume leadership roles and responsibility?
- How can existing leaders create spaces and opportunities for practitioners to recognize themselves as leaders and fulfil their leadership potential and capability?
- How can experienced leaders support practitioners in finding their feet as leaders of change in early years provision?

To develop leaders of change within settings, experienced early years leaders need to inspire, engage and encourage practitioners to view themselves as learning experts, neophyte leaders and agents of change who have the ability to exert leverage over, and own, the process of change.

Closing thoughts

One of the challenges of the current reform agenda is to create an early years workforce that is curious, eager to learn, think and improve, and capable of responding to unpredictable circumstances. When receptivity to, readiness for and responsiveness to change are embedded as an integral part of a learning organization and culture, important benefits accrue. First, lifelong learning helps develop capable early years professionals at every level who aspire to continuous improvement and innovation, and regard change as a positive driver for enhancing quality. Second, capable and well-qualified early years professionals are attracted to settings that have a reputation for the pursuit of excellence and empowerment of staff through a culture of learning and thinking. Third, capable team members who know how to learn are more efficient and productive, especially in times of change, and ultimately are more cost-effective. Finally, a culture of learning and thinking offers a pathway for capacity-building and succession planning because it provides in-house development opportunities for aspiring and potential leaders.

9

AIDE-MEMOIRE FOR LEADING CHANGE IN THE EARLY YEARS

Cherish your visions and your dreams as they are the children of your soul; the blueprints of your ultimate achievements.
Napoleon Hill

The degree to which early years practitioners are receptive, ready and responsive to pressure for complex change rests on competent leadership. Steering early years practitioners and provision through the complexities and challenges of ongoing agendas, directives and initiatives for reform and change can be testing for those who aspire to, assume or are thrust into leadership roles, especially if resistance from those involved is encountered during the process. Leading change in early years provision is founded on vision, sensitivity, patience, interpersonal competence and professional expertise. The key to successfully leading change in the early years sector is to understand and address all of the elements that contribute to the process.

Those leading change rightly operate at all levels within early years settings and, regardless of position, qualifications and experience, authentic leaders possess certain attributes, including:

- **interpersonal competence** (articulate communicators, empathic, emotionally intelligent, able to inspire and engage others with a vision);

- **curiosity** (sustained interest in learning, personal and professional growth, improving practice and professionally responsible change);

- **perceptivity** (able to read people, situations, workplace atmosphere, political climate and professional directions);

- **responsibility** (values-driven and willing to have, be, take and share accountability for improvement through change);

- **adaptability** (willing to adjust style and approach according to the needs of people, situation and context);

- **confidence about risk-taking** (willing to find and try new possibilities while balancing risks and benefits).

Clearly, there is no one right way to lead change. However, successfully leading change in the early years appears to be associated with specific key characteristics:

- communication and interpersonal competence;
- culture of ongoing learning and development;
- critical thinking and reflection;
- collaboration and collective responsibility;
- consolidation of new learning and practice into daily routine;
- conflict resolution and consensus;
- compelling vision that champions continuous quality improvement.

It is recommended that those leading any agenda or directive for reform and improvement within early years provision keep these key characteristics at the forefront of thinking when responding to pressure for change.

Change, regardless of scope and magnitude, is more likely to be achieved when those concerned understand why it is necessary, are emotionally committed to successful implementation and willingly participate and contribute. Consequently, those leading change in the early years have a responsibility to communicate and model proactive and positive attitudes and behaviours concerning engagement with change to those involved.

Although various frameworks and guidelines for effecting change are available, no one approach can or will meet different needs, or fit each and every circumstance or context. There is no formula, recipe or blueprint for success. However, those who are experienced in leading change highlight certain elements that appear to facilitate its processes and journey.

Change in early years provision is more likely to be effected when those leading it integrate many of the following activities into their own unique approach:

- **coax** practitioners to become **curious** about growth, development and improvement in self, others, early years settings and the sector;
- **captivate** practitioners' imagination and vision with ideas of possibility;
- **challenge complacency** and **confront** dogged conformity to convention and the status quo;
- **commit to** and **campaign for** professionally responsible improvement, reform and change;
- **cooperate, consult, collaborate** and work towards consensus with practitioners, other partners and stakeholders;
- **cope** with own and others' anxiety, fear, stress and other negative emotions using emotionally intelligent strategies;
- **concentrate** on facilitating the engagement and participation of, and **commend** the **contribution** of practitioners;

- **channel** collective ownership of change to practitioners;
- **combine** creative, rational, analytical and innovative thinking strategies in decision-making and problem-solving with consultation and common sense;
- **confidently** address identified issues, concerns and challenges;
- **communicate a can-do attitude** when **confronting** problems and setbacks;
- **capitalize** on unanticipated opportunities or circumstances;
- **cultivate** learning and thinking, **customize** professional development opportunities;
- **connect** practitioners with appropriate mentors and coaches;
- **champion** change, **circulate** and **celebrate** success no matter how small;
- **cultivate capability** and **consolidate capacity** by distributing leadership.

Those who competently lead change in early years engage practitioners in meaningful, relevant and constructive contribution, support and build collaborative partnerships that champion change and drive progress, improvement and achievement through the integration of people, professional and pedagogical considerations.

References

Action for Children (2008) *As Long As It Takes: A New Politics for Children*. London: Action for Children. Available at: www.actionforchildren.org.uk/media/144001/alait.pdf (accessed 28 January 2014).

Aigner, G. (2011) *Leadership Beyond Good Intentions. What It Takes to Really Make a Difference*. Crows Nest, NSW: Allen & Unwin.

Altvater, D., Godsoe, B., James, L. et al. (2005) *A Dance that Creates Equals: Unpacking Leadership Development*. New York: NYU Wagner Research Center for Leadership in Action. Available at: http://leadershiplearning.org/leadership-resources/resources-and-publications/dance-tha-creates-equals (accessed 21 November 2014).

Anning, A., Cullen, J. and Fleet, M. (2009) *Early Childhood Education, Society and Culture*, 2nd edn. London: Sage Publications.

Applebaum, L. and Paese, M. (2003) *White Paper, What senior leaders do: The nine roles of strategic leadership*. Pittsburg, PA: Development Dimensions International. Available at: www.ddiworld.com/DDIWorld/media/whitepapers/WhatSeniorLeadersDoTheNineRoles_wp_ddi.pdf?ext=.pdf (accessed 28 October 2012).

Aubrey, C. (2011) *Leading and Managing in the Early Years*, 2nd edn. London: Sage Publications.

Aubrey, C., Godfrey, R. and Harris, A. (2013) How do they manage? An investigation of early childhood leadership, *Educational Management Administration and Leadership*, 41(1): 5–29.

Baldock, P., Fitzgerald, D. and Kay, J. (2013) *Understanding Early Years Policy*, 3rd edn. London: Sage Publications.

Barratt, D.J. (2006) Leadership communication: a communication approach for senior-level managers, *Handbook of Business Strategy*, 7(1): 385–90.

Barrett, D.J. (2010) *Leadership Communication*, 3rd edn. New York: McGraw-Hill Higher Education.

Bass, M. (2000) The future of leadership in learning organizations, *Journal of Leadership Studies*, 7(3): 18–40.

Bennis, W.G. (2009) *On Becoming a Leader*. New York: Basic Books.

Beer, M. and Nohria, N. (2011) Cracking the code of change, in *Harvard Business Review, On Change*. Boston, MA: Harvard Business Review Press.

Beer, M., Eisenstat, R.A. and Spector, B. (2011) Why change programs don't produce change, in *Harvard Business Review, On Change*. Boston, MA: Harvard Business Review Press.

Bruno, H.E. (2008) *What You Need to Lead an Early Childhood Program: Emotional Intelligence in Practice*. New York: National Association for the Education of Young Children.

Burnes, B. (2004) Kurt Lewin and the planned approach to change: a re-appraisal, *Journal of Management Studies*, 41(6): 977–1002.

Campbell-Evans, G., Stamopoulos, E. and Maloney, C. (2014) Building leadership capacity in early childhood pre-service teachers, *Australian Journal of Teacher Education*, 39(5): 42–9.

Claxton, G. (2002) *Building Learning Power*. Bristol: Henleaze House.

Costly, C., Elliott, G. and Gibbs, P. (2010) *Doing Work Based Research: Approaches to Enquiry for Insider-Researchers*. London: Sage Publications.

Covey, S. (2004) *The Seven Habits of Highly Effective People*. London: Simon & Schuster.

Cummings, T.G. and Huse, E.F. (1989) *Organization Development and Change*, 4th edn. St Paul, MN: West Publishing.

Davis, G. (2012) A documentary analysis of the use of leadership and change theory in changing practice in early years settings, *Early Years: International Journal of Research*, 32(3): 266–76.

Daws, J.E. (2005) Teachers and students as co-learners: possibilities and problems, *Journal of Educational Enquiry*, 6(1): 110–25.

Deakin, E. (2007) The role of meaningful dialogue in early childhood education leadership, *Australasian Journal of Early Childhood*, 32(1): 38–46.

Department for Children, Schools and Families (2010) *Challenging Practice to Further Improve Learning, Playing and Interacting in the Early Years Foundation Stage*. Nottingham: DCSF Publications. Available at: www.ndna.org.uk/Resources/NDNA/Generic%20Folders%202/10/20.%20Challenging%20Practice.pdf (accessed 10 October 2013).

Drucker, P. (2007) *The Essential Drucker*, Classic Drucker Collection. Oxford: Butterworth-Heinemann.

Dunlop, A. (2008) A literature review on leadership in the early years. Available at: www.ltscotland.org.uk/Images/leadershipreview_tcm4-499140.doc (accessed 20 October 2011).

Dunlop, A. (2012) Foreword, in R. McDowall Clark and J. Murray, *Reconceptualizing Leadership in the Early Years*. Maidenhead: Open University Press.

Ebbeck, M. and Waniganayake, M. (2003) *Early Childhood Professionals: Leading Today and Tomorrow*. Sydney: MacLennan & Petty.

Edwards, A. (2009) *Improving Inter-Professional Collaborations: Multi-Agency Working for Children's Well-being*. London: Routledge.

Eggers, J.T. (2011) *Research Notes, Psychological safety influences relationship behavior*. Available at: www.aca.org/research/pdf/ResearchNotes_Feb2011.pdf (accessed 23 February 2013).

Elliot, A. (2012) Embracing change in early childhood, *Every Child*, 8(4). Available at: www.earlychildhoodaustralia.org.au/every_child_magazine/every_child_index/editorial-embracing-change-in-early-childhood.html (accessed 10 May 2013).

Farrago, J. and Skyrme, D. (1995) The learning organization. Available at: www.skyrme.com/insights/3lrnorg.htm (accessed 4 April 2013).

Fenech, M. (2006) The impact of regulatory environment on early childhood professional practice and job satisfaction: a review of conflicting discourses, *Australasian Journal of Early Childhood*, 31(2): 49–57.

Fullan, M. (2001) *Leading in a Culture of Change*. New York: Jossey-Bass.

Garvey, D. and Lancaster, A. (2010) *Leadership and Quality in Early Years and Playwork*. London: National Children's Bureau.

Garvin, D.A. and Roberto, M.A. (2011) Change through persuasion, *in Harvard Business Review, On Change*. Boston, MA: Harvard Business Review Press.

Georgeson, J. and Payler, J. (2013) *International Perspectives on Early Childhood Education and Care*. Maidenhead: Open University Press.

Goleman, D. (1996) *Emotional Intelligence: Why It Can Matter More Than IQ*. London: Bloomsbury.

Goleman, D. (2002) Becoming a resonant leader, *Harvard Management Update*, 7(7): 4–6.

Glouberman, S. and Zimmerman, B. (2002) *Complicated and Complex Systems: What Would Successful Reform of Medicare Look Like?* Commission of Future Healthcare in Canada. Available at: www.healthandeverything.org/files/GloubermanE. pdf (accessed 16 March 2013).

Greany, T. and Rodd, J. (2003) *Creating a Learning to Learn School.* Stafford: Network Educational Press.

Grogan, M. and Shakeshaft, C. (2009) Conscious leadership in a political world, in H. Sobehart (ed.) *Women Leading Education Across the Continents: Sharing the Spirit. Fanning the Flame.* Lanham, MD: Rowman & Littlefield Publications.

Hallet, E. (2012) *The Reflective Early Years Practitioner.* London: Sage Publications.

Harris, A. and Lambert, L. (2003) *Building Leadership Capacity for School Improvement.* Maidenhead: Open University Press.

Harris, A. and Spillane, J. (2008) Distributed leadership through the looking glass, *Management in Education,* 22(1): 31–4.

Health Promotion Unit (2007) *Stages of Behaviour Change: Queensland Stay On Your Feet® Community Good Practice Toolkit.* Brisbane: Division of Chief Health Officer, Queensland Health. Available at: www.health.qld.gov.au/stayonyourfeet/ documents/33331.pdf (accessed 12 October 2012).

Heifetz, R. (1994) *Leadership Without Easy Answers.* Boston, MA: Harvard University Press.

Heifetz, R.A. and Linsky, M. (2011) A survival guide for leaders, in *Harvard Business Review, On Change.* Boston, MA: Harvard Business Review Press.

Hemp, P. and Stewart, T.A. (2011) Leading change when business is good: an interview with Samuel J. Palmisano, in *Harvard Business Review, On Change.* Boston, MA: Harvard Business Review Press.

Hood, M. (2012) Partnerships – working together in early childhood settings, *Early Childhood Australia,* Research in Practice Series, 1(19). Available at: www. earlychildhoodaustralia.org.au/pdf/rips/RIP1201_sample.pdf (accessed 24 October, 2013).

Hopkins, D. (2008) *A Teacher's Guide to Classroom Research,* 4th edn. Philadelphia, PA: Open University Press.

Hujala, E. (2013) Contextually defined leadership, in E. Hujala, M. Waniganayake and J. Rodd (eds) *Researching Leadership in Early Childhood Education.* Tampere, Finland: Tampere University Press.

Hydon, C. and I'Anson, C. (2009) Swimming between the flags, *Reflections* (Gowrie Australia), Summer, 37: 4–5.

Johnson, D.W. (2013) *Reaching Out. Interpersonal Effectiveness and Self-actualization,* 11th international edn. London: Pearson.

Kagan, S.L. (1999) The more things change, the more they stay the same: fact or fiction? From Our President, *Young Children,* 54(1): 2, 65.

Kahane, A. (2004) *Solving Tough Problems.* San Francisco: Berrett-Koehler Publishers.

Keegan, S. (2011) *The Death of Business Management – Introducing Generation Z,* Kindle edn. Available at: www.amazon.co.uk/Death-Business-Management-Introducingebook/dp/B005PG49RE (accessed 12 December 2013).

Kezar, A.J. (2001) *Understanding and Facilitating Organizational Change in the 21st Century. Recent Research and Conceptualizations.* New York: John Wiley & Sons.

Kingdon, Z. and Gourd, J. (2014) *Early Years Policy. The Impact of Practice.* London: Routledge.

Knoster, T., Villa, R. and Thousand, J. (2000) A framework for thinking about systems change, in R. Villa and J. Thousand, (eds) *Restructuring for Caring and Effective Education: Piecing the Puzzle Together*. Baltimore, MD: Paul Brookes Publishing Co.

Kotter, J.P. (1990) *A Force for Change. How Leadership Differs from Management*. New York: Free Press.

Kotter, J.P. (1999) *John P. Kotter on What Leaders Really Do*. Boston, MA: Harvard Business School Press.

Kotter, J.P. (2003) *Leading Change*. Boston, MA: Harvard Business School Press.

Kotter, J.P. (2011) Leading change: why transformation efforts fail, in *Harvard Business Review, On Change*. Boston, MA: Harvard Business Review Press.

Kotter, J.P. (2012) *Leading Change*. Boston, MA: Harvard Business Review Press.

Kouzes, J.M. and Posner, B.Z. (2012) *The Leadership Challenge*, 5th edn. San Francisco: Jossey-Bass.

Kremenitzer, J.P. and Miller, R. (2008) Are you a highly qualified emotionally intelligent early childhood educator? *Young Children*, July: 106–12.

Kübler-Ross, E. and Kessler, D. (2005) *On Grief and Grieving: Finding the Meaning of Grief Through the Five Stages of Loss*. London: Simon & Schuster.

Kwon, Y. (2002) Changing curriculum for early childhood education in England, *Early Childhood Research and Practice*, 4(2). Available at: http://ecrp.uiuc.edu/v4n2/kwon.html (accessed 16 May 2013).

Leeson, C. (2010) Leadership in early childhood settings, in R. Parker-Rees, C. Leeson, J. Willan and J. Savage (eds) *Early Childhood Studies*. 3rd edn. Exeter: Learning Matters.

Lindon, J. (2010) *Reflective Practice and Early Years Professionalism: Linking Theory and Practice*. Abingdon: Hodder Education.

Lindon, J. and Lindon, L. (2012) *Leadership and Early Years Professionalism: Theory and Practice*. Abingdon: Hodder Education.

Lochrie, M. (2009) *Lifelong Learning and the Early Years*. Leicester: National Institute of Adult Continuing Education.

Lombardo, M. and Elchinger, R. (1996) *The Career Architect Development Planner*. Minneapolis, MN: Lominger.

Macfarlane, K., Cartmel, J. and Nolan, A. (2011) *Developing and Sustaining Pedagogical Leadership in Early Childhood Education and Care Professionals, Final Report*. Strawberry Hills, NSW: Australian Learning and Teaching Council. Available at: www.olt.gov.au/system/files/.../LE8_823_Macfarlane_Report_2011 (accessed 20 March 2013).

Maslow, A. (1970) *Motivation and Personality*. New York: Harper & Row.

Mathers, S., Singler, R. and Karemaker, A. (2012) *Improving Quality in the Early Years: A Comparison of Perspectives and Measures*. Oxford: Daycare Trust and University of Oxford.

McDowall Clark, R. (2012) I've never thought of myself as a leader but . . .': the early years professional and catalytic leadership, *European Early Childhood Education Research Journal*, 20(3): 391–401.

McDowall Clark, R. and Murray, J. (2012) *Reconceptualizing Leadership in the Early Years*. Maidenhead: Open University Press.

McNiff, J. and Whitehead, J. (2009) *Doing and Writing Action Research*. London: Sage Publications.

Miller, L. and Cable, C. (2011) *Professionalization, Leadership and Management in the Early Years*. London: Sage Publications.

Miller, L., Drury, R. and Cable, C. (2012) *Extending Professional Practice in the Early Years*. London: Sage Publications.

Moss Kantor, R. (1999) The enduring skills of change leaders, *Leader to Leader*, 13: 15–22.

Moyles, J. (2006) *Effective Leadership and Management in the Early Years*. Maidenhead: Open University Press.

Moyles, J, Payler, J. and Georgeson, J. (2014) *Early Years Foundations: Critical Issues*. Maidenhead: Open University Press.

National Union of Teachers (2013) *NUT Early Years Foundation Stage Profile, Advice and Guidance for Members*, January. Available at: www.teachers.org.uk/node/15517 (accessed 3 March 2014).

Nutbrown, C. (2012) *The Nutbrown Report, Review of Early Education and Childcare Qualifications: Interim Report*. Available at: www.gov.uk/government/publications/review-of-early-education-and-childcare-qualifications-interim-report (accessed 19 December 2013).

Oberhuemer, P., Schreyer, I. and Neuman, M.J. (2010) *Professionals in Early Childhood Education and Care Systems. European Profiles and Perspectives*. Opladen and Farmington Hills: Anne Budrich Publishers.

O'Connor, C. (2012) *Successful Leadership In a Week*, 4th edn. London: Hodder Education.

O'Gorman, L. and Hand, L. (2013) Looking back and looking forward: exploring distributed leadership with Queensland prep teachers, *Australasian Journal of Early Childhood*, 38(3). Available at: www.earlychildhoodaustralia.org.au/australian_journal_of_early_childhood.html (accessed 3 March 2014).

O'Sullivan, J. (2009) *Leadership Skills in the Early Years: Making a Difference*. London: Network Continuum Publications.

OECD (Organization for Economic Cooperation and Development) (2012) *Starting Strong III: A Quality Toolbox for Early Childhood Education and Care*. Paris: OECD Publishing. Available at: www.oecd.org/edu/school/startingstrongiii-aqualitytoolboxforearlychildhoodeducationandcare.htm (accessed 25 February 2014).

Olsen, E.E. and Eoyang, G.H. (2001) *Facilitating Organizational Change: Lessons from Complexity Science*. New York: Jossey-Bass/Pfeiffer.

Ord, K., Mane, J., Smortj, S. et al. (2013) *Developing Pedagogical Leadership in Early Childhood Education*. Wellington: New Zealand Childcare Association. Available at: https://nzca.ac.nz/assets/Uploads/Member-resources/Developing-Pedagogical-leadership.pdf (accessed 17 January 2014).

Paige-Smith, A. and Craft, A. (2011) *Developing Reflective Practice in the Early Years*, 2nd edn. Maidenhead: Open University Press.

Painter, A. (2014) Core values, *Royal Society of Arts Journal*, 1: 39–41.

Proschaska, J.O. and DiClemente, C.C. (1988) Towards a comprehensive model of change, in W. Millert and N. Heather (eds) *Treating Addictive Behaviors*. New York: Plenum Press.

Puffett, N. (2013) Leadership instability linked to children's provision failings, *Children and Young People Now*, 15 October 2013. Available at: www.cypnow.co.uk/cyp/news/1119148/child-protection-failings-linked-leadership-instability (accessed 28 October 2013).

Reed, M. and Canning, N. (2012) *Implementing Quality Improvement and Change in the Early Years*. London: Sage Publications.

Rodd, J. (2013a) *Leadership in Early Childhood, The Pathway to Professionalism*, 4th edn. Crows Nest, NSW: Allen & Unwin.

Rodd, J. (2013b) Reflecting on the pressures, pitfalls and possibilities for examining leadership in early childhood within a cross-national research collaboration, in E. Hujala, M. Waniganayake and J. Rodd (eds) *Researching Leadership in Early Childhood Education*. Tampere, Finland: Tampere University Press.

Rodgers, A. and Wilmot, E. (2011) *Inclusion and Diversity in the Early Years*. London: Practical Pre-School Books.

Rogers, C. (1967) *Freedom to Learn: A View of What Education Might Become*. Columbus, OH: Charles Merrill Publishing Company.

Rogers, E.M. (2003) *The Diffusion of Innovators*, 5th edn. New York: Free Press.

Rose, J., Fuller, M., Gilbert, L. and Palmer, S. (2011) Transformative empowerment: stimulating transformation in early years practice, *Learning and Teaching in Higher Education*, 5: 56–72.

Russell, D. (2002) *Carl Rogers the Quiet Revolutionary: An Oral History*. Roseville, CA: Penmarin Books.

Schein, E. H. (1988) *Organizational Psychology*, 3rd edn. London: Prentice Hall.

Scherer, Z. and Efoise, M. (2013) *Y'd Awake: Understanding and Managing Generation Y*, Kindle edn. Available at: www.amazon.co.uk/YD-Awake-Understanding-Generation-ebook/dp/B00BELPCHU (accessed 14 November 2013).

Schermerhorn, J.R., Hunt, J.G. and Osborn, R.N. (2005) *Organizational Behavior*, 9th edn. New York: John Wiley & Sons Inc.

Schutz, W. (1994) *The Human Element: Productivity, Self-esteem and the Bottom Line*. San Francisco: Jossey-Bass.

Senge, P. (2006) *The Fifth Discipline: The Art and Practice of the Learning Organization*, 2nd edn. New York: Doubleday.

Senior, B. and Swales, S. (2010) *Organizational Change*, 4th edn. Harlow: Pearson Education Ltd.

Sharp, C., Lord, P., Handscomb, G. et al. (2012) *Highly Effective Leadership in Children's Centres*. Nottingham: National College for School Leadership.

Sims, M. (2011) What does being an early childhood 'teacher' mean in tomorrow's world of children and family services? Available at: www.pc.gov.au/__data/assets/pdf_file/0003/106698/sub002-attachment.pdf (accessed 2 February 2014)

Siraj-Blatchford, I. and Hallet, E. (2013) *Effective and Caring Leadership in the Early Years*. London: Sage Publications.

Snow, C.E. and Van Hemel, S.B. (2008) *National Research Council, Early Childhood Assessment: Why, What, and How?* Washington, DC: National Academies Press.

Stacey, M. 2009, *Teamwork and Collaboration in Early Years Settings*. London: Sage Publications.

Stagl, H. (2011) Six roles of a leader during change. Available at: www.enclaria.com/2011/10/06/six-roles-of-a-leader-during-change/(accessed 27 October 2012).

Stamopoulos, E. (2011) Building early childhood leadership capacity through professional knowledge, an interpretative lens, courage and relational trust, *Reflections*, Spring, 44: 11–13.

Stoll, L., Fink, D. and Earl, L. (2002) *It's About Learning (and it's about time)*. London: RoutledgeFalmer.

Stonehouse, A. and Gonzales-Mena, J. (2004) *Making Links: A Collaborative Approach to Planning and Practice*. NSW: Pademelon Press.

Su, A.J. and Wilkins, M.M. (2013) *Own the Room: Discover Your Signature Voice. How to Master Your Leadership Presence*. Harvard, MA: Harvard Business Review Press.

Sullivan, D. (2010) Welcome the change coming soon to your life, *Exchange, The Early Childhood Leader's Magazine Since 1978*, 192(March–April): 8–11.

Taylor, M. and Senge, P. (2014) Seats of learning, *Royal Society of Arts Journal*, 1: 10–15.

Te Kopae Piripono (2006) *Ngā takohanga e wha. The four responsibilities*. Available at: www.lead.ece.govt.nz/CentresOfInnovation/COIDocsAndResources/SrvcSpecificDocsAndResources/NgaTakohangaeWhaTheFourResponsibilities.htm (accessed 17 January 2014).

Unison in Early Years (2013) Changes to early years provision, *Newsletter for Early Years Workers*, Spring, 1–3. Available at: http://content.durham.gov.uk/PDFRepository/UNISONEarlyYearsNewsletterApril2013.pdf (accessed 3 March, 2014).

Urban, M., Vandenbroeck, M. and Peeters, J. (2011) *CoRe Final Report. Competence Requirements in Early Childhood Education and Care*. London and Ghent: University of East London, Cass School of Education and University of Ghent, Department of Social Work.

Van de Ven, A.H and Poole, M.S. (1995) Explaining development and change in organizations, *Academy of Management Review*, 20(3): 510-40.

Waniganayake, M. (2013) Leadership careers in early childhood: Finding your way through chaos and serendipity into strategic planning, in E. Hujala, M. Waniganayake and J. Rodd (eds) *Researching Leadership in Early Childhood Education*. Tampere, Finland: Tampere University Press.

Warrick, D.D. (2009) Developing organizational change champions, *OD Practitioner*, 41(1): 14–19.

Whalley, M. and Allen, S. (2011) *Leading Practice in Early Years Settings*. Exeter: Learning Matters.

Wong, S., Press, F. and Sumison, J. (2012) Supporting professional development in integrated early childhood services: a resource for leaders developed for the Professional Support Coordinators Alliance (PSCA). Available at: www.psctas.org.au/wp-content/uploads/2012/07/supporting-professional-development-in-integrated-context-web-Final.pdf (accessed 8 January 2014).

Yukl, G. (1999) An evaluation of conceptual weaknesses in transformational and charismatic leadership theories, *The Leadership Quarterly*, 10(2): 285–305.

Author Index

Action for Children, 1
Aigner, G., 8, 28, 31, 123
Altvater, D., Godsoe, B., James, L. et al., 33
Anning, A., Cullen, J. and Fleet, M., 27
Applebaum, L. and Paese, M., 40
Aubrey, C., 8, 30, 97, 117-8
Aubrey, C., Godfrey, R. and Harris, A., 32

Baldock, P., Fitzgerald, D. and Kay, J., 27
Barrett, D.J., 75-6, 78
Bass, M., 6
Bennis, W., 50, 88
Beer, M. and Nohria, N., 24
Beer, M., Eisenstat, R.A. and Spector, B., 25
Bruno, H.E., 83
Burnes, B., 19

Campbell-Evans, G., Stamopoulos, E. and Maloney, C., 134
Claxton, G., 127
Costly, C., Elliott, G. and Gibbs, P., 23
Covey, S., 61, 88
Cummings, T. G. and Huse, E. F., 19

Davis, G., 14
Daws, J.E., 108
Deakin, E., 76
Department for Children, Schools and Families, 69
Drucker, P., 49
Dunlop, A., xii, 16-7, 30, 35, 76, 104

Ebbeck, M. and Waniganayake, M., 49, 65, 91, 99
Edwards, A., 32
Eggers, J.T., 63
Elliot, A., 91

Farrago, J. and Skyrme, D., 128
Fenech, M., 135
Fullan, M., 5, 13, 132, 135

Garvey, D. and Lancaster, A., 30
Garvin, D.A. and Roberto, M.A., 24, 90
Georgeson, J. and Payler, J., xii
Goleman, D., 83
Glouberman, S. and Zimmerman, B., 51
Greany, T. and Rodd, J., 129
Grogan, M. and Shakeshaft, C., 108

Hallet, E., 62
Harris, A. and Lambert, L., 132, 135
Harris, A. and Spillane, J., 37
Health Promotion Unit, 21
Heifetz, R., 123
Heifetz, R.A. and Linsky, M., 91
Hemp, P. and Stewart, T.A., 63
Hood, M., 62, 64-5
Hopkins, D., 23
Hujala, E., 31
Hydon, C. and I'Anson, C., 122-3

Johnson, D.W., 62, 71, 77-9, 81

Kagan, S.L., 1, 13
Kahane, A., 124
Keegan, S., 29
Kezar, A.J., 14
Kingdon, Z. and Gourd, J., 8
Knoster, T., Villa, R. and Thousand, J., 54
Kotter, J.P., 15, 21-2, 47-9, 76, 89
Kouzes, J.M. and Posner, B.Z., 36, 46, 132
Kremenitzer, J.P. and Miller, R., 84
Kubler-Ross, E. and Kessler, D., 95
Kwon, Y., 51

Leeson, C., 36
Lindon, J., 30
Lindon, J. and Lindon, L., 8, 46
Lochrie, M., 122
Lombardo, M. and Elchinger, R., 128

Macfarlane, K., Cartmel, J. and Nolan, A., 25
Maslow, A., 57, 122

Mathers, S., Singler, R. and
   Karemaker, A., 30
McDowall Clark, R., 11
McDowall Clark, R. and Murray, J., 8,
   30, 107
McNiff, J. and Whitehead, J., 20
Miller, L. and Cable, C., 91
Miller, L., Drury, R. and Cable, C., 8
Moss Kantor, R., 8
Moyles, J., 30, 36, 63, 104
Moyles, J., Payler, J. and Georgeson, J., 3

National Union of Teachers, 94
Nutbrown, C., 28, 122

Oberhuemer, P., Schreyer, I. and
   Neuman, M.J., xii
O'Connor, C., 3, 63, 75
O'Gorman, L. and Hand, L., 109
O'Sullivan, J., 78, 83
OECD, 6, 8
Olsen, E.E., and Eoyang, G.H., 18
Ord, K., Mane, J., Smortj, S. et al., 33,
   108, 121, 134

Paige-Smith, A. and Craft, A., 107
Painter, A., 121
Proschaska, J.O. and DiClemente, C.C., 21
Puffett, N., 30-1, 96, 118

Reed, M. and Canning, N., 2, 8, 30
Rodd, J., xii, 7, 8, 13, 30-4, 36-7, 46, 48,
   57, 78, 118
Rodgers, A. and Wilmot, E., 51
Rogers, C., 133
Rogers, E.M., 113
Rose, J., Fuller, M., Gilbert, L. et al., 6
Russell, D., 133

Schein, E. H., 19
Scherer, Z. and Efoise, M., 29
Schermerhorn, J.R., Hunt, J.G. and
   Osborn, R.N., 99
Schutz, W., 96
Senge, P., 14, 125-6, 132
Senior, B. and Swales, S., 20
Sharp, C., Lord, P., Handscomb, G.
   et al., 30, 32, 70, 83, 115, 124, 134
Sims, M., 62, 78
Siraj-Blatchford, I. and Hallet, E., 40, 48,
   76, 83, 108, 132
Snow C.E. and Van Hemel, S.B., 8
Stacey, M., 115
Stagl, H., 39
Stamopoulos, E., 64, 91
Stoll, L., Fink, D. and Earl, L., 135
Stonehouse, A. and Gonzales-Mena, J.,
   124
Su, A. J. and Wilkins, M. M., 35
Sullivan, D., 28

Taylor, M. and Senge, P., 125
Te Kopae Piripono, 134

Unison in Early Years, 91
Urban, M., Vandenbroek, M. and
   Peeters, J., xii, 31, 46, 51, 122, 134

Van de Ven, A.H and Poole, M.S., 14

Waniganayake, M., 32
Warrick, D.D., 114
Whalley, M and Allen, S., 91-2
Wong, S., Press, F. and Sumison, J.,
   132

Yukl, G., 35

Subject Index

accountability, 4, 77, 108-9, 111, 134
action, 94, 108, 110, 131
  planning, 19, 23, 24, 34, 42, 56, 57, 58,
      88, 89, 113
  research, 20, 22, 23
  systematic, 19
advocacy, 39, 41, 42, 103, 112
assertion, 36, 70, 82, 97
avoidance, 98

beliefs, *see* values
'big picture', 53, 88, 90, 94, 106, 115, 126,
      see also vision
bullying, 67
burnout, 59, 122

capacity building, 133-6
change, 11-26
  adaptive, 123-4, 128
  agenda, 2, 3, 6, 9, 16-7, 26-8, 59, 72, 92,
      104, 115, 119, 128, 138
  agents, xii, 51, 90
  approaches to, 5, 27
  attitudes to, 13, 108
  barriers to, 7, 19, 21, 24-5, 42, 69, 105
  benefits of, 5, 13, 16-7
  bureaucratic, 123
  catalyst for, 11, 132
  challenges, 8-9
  champion, 7, 23-4, 42, 105, 107, 112,
      114, 118-19, 138
  collective responsibility, 5, 7, 107-19
  commitment to, 13, 15
  complex, 1, 5-6, 12-13, 15, 17, 18, 25,
      29, 46, 50-9, 96, 100, 124
    elements of, 54-9
  consensus, 8, 54, 56, 59
  cycles of, 20, 22
  definition of, 11, 12, 17
  diagnosing, 20
  dimensions, 14, 17, 18
  dysfunctional strategies, 24
  emotions about, 5
  evaluating, 9, 10, 23, 52, 58-9
  failure of, 8, 15, 24, 76, 89, 112
  features of, 13

  forces, 12, 20
  goals of, 2, 5, 8
  history of, 2, 92
  implementation, 15, 23, 24, 25, 30, 52,
      57, 63, 71, 76, 83, 89, 115, 118
  instigation of, 3, 6, 15
  as learning cycle, 22-3
  magnitude of, 1, *see also* scope
  models, 18-22
  monitoring, 23, 52
  motivational orientations, 113-15
    early adopters, 113, 114, 118
    early majority, 113-4
    innovators, 113
    laggards, 113
    late majority, 113-4
  need for, 2-3, 6, 21
  need assessment, 23
  negative attitudes, 15, 95
  objects of, 12
  obstacles, *see* barriers to
  ownership, 54, 73, 88, 110, 117,
      125, 138
  pace, 5, 6, 27, 57, 93, 124
  paradigms, 14
  parameters, 16
  personal needs, 96
  planning for, 15, 17
  pressure for, 1, 2, 4, 10, 12, 124
  proactive attitudes, 6, 15, 27, 97, 104,
      105, 112, 138
  process of, 3, 6, 15, 18-20, 22-4, 28, 42,
      62, 105, 112, 118-19
  readiness for, 2, 4, 6, 17, 23, 56, 75,
      112, 121, 122, 137
  reasons for, 5, 13, 15, 75, 87, 105
  receptive to, 2, 4, 6-7, 17, 69, 75, 91-106,
      110, 112, 115, 121, 122, 137
  resistance to, 5, 13, 15, 17, 23, 24, 28,
      77, 83, 91-106, 112, 131, 137
  rewards, 19
  risk taking, 19, 41, 48, 95, 124, 137
  scope, 5, 12, 14, 15, 17, 27, 93, 124
  short-term wins, 22
  simple, 1, 16-18, 51
  stages, 14, 18, 21, 22, 42

change (*continued*)
  stages of grieving, 95-6
  steps in cycles, 20-1
  sustainability, 7, 12, 25, 76, 111, 115,
      118, 119, 121-136
  technical, 123, 128
  terminology, 46
  theories, 14, *see also* paradigms
  threat of, 5, 93
  timeline, 6, 23, 112
  timing, 14, 105
  tipping point, 95
  transformational, 17, 124
  types, 12, 15, 51-2, 115
  vision for, 11, 13, 22, 88-90
climate, 4, 32, 62, 70, 72, 105, 127, 131
coaching, 24, 38, 125, 130, 136, 138
co-option, 102
collaboration, 2, 7, 8, 40, 71, 72, 77,
      98-119, 135, 138
  benefits of, 117
  in conflict resolution, 98, 103
  in teams, 34, 37, 111, 113, 115-6
  responsibility, 5
  role of leader, 118-9
  strategies for, 118
  teamwork, 7, 72, 107, 115, 118
  win-win, 98
collective responsibility, 4, 40, 99,
      107-17, 134, 138
comfort zone, 13, 17, 71, 92-5
communication, 24, 29, 34, 40, 62-3,
      75-90, 103, 105, 112, 114-15,
      118, 125, 130
  benefits of skills, 77, 86
  breakdown, 76
  definition, 77
  electronic, 75, 77, 86
  face-to-face, 75, 77, 86
  goals, 78
  medium, 83, 85
  roadblocks, 84-6
  skills, 82-3
  style, 83
  understanding of, 85
competition, 98
compromise, 98
confidentiality, 66-7, 68-9, 111
conflict, 38, 62, 84, 87, 91-106
  definition of, 91-2

  personal style, 104
  reaction to, 92, 95-9
    accommodation, 98
    avoidance, 98
    collaboration, 98
    competition, 98
    compromise, 98
  reasons for, 94
  resolution, 25, 70, 73, 77, 83, 111
    strategies, 99-104, 138
      advocacy, 103
      education and communication,
        99-100
      explicit and implicit coercion,
        102-3
      facilitation and support, 100-1
      manipulation and co-option, 101-2
      negotiation and agreement, 101
      participation and involvement,
        100
      problem resolution, 103-4
consensus, 8, 54, 73, 138
context, 14, 31, 138
  economic, political, social, 1, 3, 4,
      7, 51
creativity, 19, 28, 64, 71, 99, 108, 117,
      122
culture, 15, 25, 30, 32, 34, 84, 86, 107
  of learning, 52, 113, 121-36, 138
  of settings, 4

decision-making, 34, 37, 40, 51, 70, 72,
      73, 77, 82, 103, 108, 110, 138
delegation, 40, 53, 59, 73, 82, 87, 105,
      109, 116
dialogue, 70, 76, 88-9, 93, 101, 108, 110,
      114, 117, 132
distributed leadership, *see* leadership,
      distributed
diversity, 27, 29, 70, 73, 84, 86, 121

education and communication, 99-100,
      103
emotional intelligence, 5, 36, 70, 83-4,
      92, 97, 98, 135, 138
ethics, 3, 38, 43, 66, 71, 84, 85, 89
evaluation, 54-8

facilitation and support, 100-1
fear and anxiety, 71-2

feedback, 19, 67, 73, 78, 81-8, 127
fiscal constraints, 4, 30
friendships, 65-9, *see also* professional
    relationships

generations, 29

hierarchical authority, 24, 109
hierarchy of needs, 57
honesty, 36, 63
horizontal violence, *see* bullying

imagination, 8
incentives, 54-7, 101
inclusion, 73
informal leadership, 4
innovation, 13, 28, 64, 71, 99, 117, 124,
    125
inspiration, 11, 36
interpersonal, 61-90
    abilities, 70
    communication, 62, 75-90
    competence, 37, 72-4, 137-8
    issues, 71-2
    relationships, 34, 61-75, 105, 110, 112
    skills, 62, 69, 83

leadership, 8, 45-59
    activities, 52, 138-9
    and change, 49-50
    and quality, 30-5, 45-59
    aspiration, 3, 133, 137
    attributes, 3, 13, 35-7, 39, 42, 70-1, 122,
        137-8
    authentic, 12, 15, 27-43, 63, 102, 127,
        130, 132, 137-8
    autocratic, 127
    beliefs, 29
    calibre, 35
    capability, 34, 73-4, 110, 124, 133, 136,
        138
    capacity, 30-3, 110, 124, 133-6, 138
    caring, 40
    challenges for, 8-9
    charismatic, 35
    choice, 31
    collaborative, 40
    collective, 40, 108, *see also*
        distributed
    context, 31, 42, 116

definition, 13, 29, 31, 32, 33, 39, 40, 47,
    40-50, 75
dimensions, 53
distributed, 15, 32, 37, 40, 41, 46, 53,
    108, 111, 116, 119, 134-6, 138
engagement with, 7
features of, 13
focus, 3, 53
functions, 31, 52
informal, 4
models, 35, 54-9
orientation, 3, 32, 46, 49-50
participation, 3
partnerships, 23
pedagogical, 53, 134
positional, xii, 3, 4, 29, 31, 41, 46
potential, 3, 30, 107, 110, 135, 136
presence, 35-7
responsibilities, xiii, 7, 15, 32-3, 108,
    111, 133-4
right, xiii, 31, 135
roles, xiii, 3, 32-3, 39-42, 111, 133, 137
skills, 37-9
spaces, 33, 136
strategic, 40-1, 53
styles, 34, 37
succession, 134, 135
transformational, 43, 49
visionary, 48
learning, 3, 18, 19, 25, 28, 38, 40-1, 92, 99,
    108, 111, 115, 117, 121-36
    and change, 3, 133
    and leadership, 38, 132-61
    collaborative, 17, 133
    co-learning, 130
    culture, *see* culture of learning
    cycles of, 22-5
    focus, 131
    impact of, 130
    lifelong, 4, 25, 29, 37, 73, 105, 122
    organization, 125-6, 129
    roles of leaders, 127, 130
    to learn, 126, 128-9
    styles, 130
    types of, 129-9
    zone, 17, 122, 132
listening, 73
    active, 72, 78-9
    effective, 80
    obstacles to, 80-1

listening (*continued*)
  reflective, *see* active
  skills, 80

management, 3, 46-9
  definition, 47, 49
  differences with leadership, 3, 46-7, 50
  functions, 50
  orientation, 41, 49-50
manipulation and co-option, 101-2
mentoring, 3, 24, 38, 40, 42, 73, 125, 130, 136, 138
micromanagement, 24, 40, 127
mission, 73, 105
mood, 84, 86
motivation, 19, 24, 25, 38, 48, 59, 63, 73, 96, 117, 124, 131

negotiation, 70, 73, 82, 87
  and agreement, 101
networking, 3, 73, 125
networks, 62, 97, 105, 117

obstacles, *see* barriers to
opposition, *see* change, resistance
organizational theory, 8
ownership, 54, 73, 88, 110, 117, 125, 138

paralinguistics, 78
participation and involvement, 100, 103
partnership, 105, 107-19
pedagogy, 3, 132
perceptions, 5, 28, 81, 84, 86, 92
perceptivity, 137
performance
personal attributes, 5
personal benefits/costs, 5
personal control, 96-7
personal narratives, 119
personal needs, 96
planning, 10, 17
power with, 28, 32
proactive receptivity, 91-106
problem-solving, 5, 24, 37, 40, 70, 72, 73, 77, 82, 87, 99, 103, 124, 125, 127, 138
professional, 8
  boundaries, 66-9
  culture, 112, 125

development, 9, 22, 62, 129, 130, 131, 136, 138
expectations, 68, 72-3
growth, 121
learning, 62
identity, 19, 25, 38, 115, 124
issues, 3
maturity, 13
philosophy, 6, 102
relationships, 64-9, 79, 83, 113
respect, 66
responsibility, 17, 27, 38, 67, 127
terminology, xii-iii
psychological safety, 19, 62, 64, 67, 73, 95-6

qualifications, xii, 11, 12, 30, 31, 122
quality improvement, 2, 4, 6, 7, 8, 11, 26, 38, 52, 84, 92-3, 103, 117, 122, 130, 135, 138

receiving messages, 70, 78-80
reflection, 19, 22, 23, 25, 28, 34, 105, 113, 117, 122, 132, 138
relationships, 28, 31, 34, 41, 52, 61-75, 86, 108, *see also* interpersonal
  collaborative, 11, 66
  turbulent, 116
resilience, 13, 36, 52, 62, 126
resistance, 5, 91-106
  definition of, 92
  overcoming, 96-104
  reasons for, 94
respect, 7, 16, 66
response alternatives, 81-2
  evaluative, 81
  interpretative, 81
  probing, 81
  supportive, 81
  understanding, 81-2
resources, 9, 24, 27, 47, 55, 57, 59, 61, 105, 113, 117
retention, 30, 96, 118, 124
risk-taking, 19, 41, 48, 95, 124, 137
rustout, 122

self-awareness, 73, 104
self-blame, 71-2
self-esteem, 19, 57, 97, 127

self-reflection, 34
self-talk, 72
sending messages, 70, 78-82, 85-86
shadowing, 130
shared leadership, *see* leadership, distributed
shyness, 71-2
social capital, 61
staff development, 9, *see also* professional
staff turnover, *see* retention
stakeholders, 5, 8, 12, 15, 19, 21, 34, 42, 71, 77, 87, 124
status quo, 17, 41, 42, 47, 94, 123, 138
stress, 7, 13, 28, 52, 59, 76, 86, 93, 112, 116, 138
  levels, 62, 72, 79
  management, 70, 105
  reduction, 77, 83, 96-7
sustainability, 12, 121-36

Te Kopae Piripono, 134-5
teams, *see* collaboration
teamwork, 24, 25, 40, 62, 64, 70, 72, 83, 107-19, 125, 127, 130
technology, 12, 15

thinking, 5, 7, 25, 34, 37, 72, 73, 75, 117, 121, 124, 125, 128, 138
tipping point, 95
training, 3, 4, 5, 22, 105, 127, 129, 130, 136
transformation, 1, 6, 13, 48, 115, 121, 125
trust, 7, 16, 24, 25, 34, 36, 62, 63, 64, 65, 72, 77, 86, 102, 110, 111, 125, 130, 132
  definition, 63

understanding response, 81-2

values, 3, 32, 33, 34, 36, 40, 41, 43, 73, 84, 90, 110, 111
vision, 11, 13, 22, 23, 25, 34, 36, 40, 41, 43, 47, 54, 59, 65, 73, 75, 77, 87, 111, 112, 115, 118, 126, 138
  communicating, 22, 24, 54, 88-90, 105
  definition, 54, 88
  features of, 89

workforce, 2, 29, 33, 122, 123, 125
workplace context, 5, 11, 17
workplace culture, 4, 7, 13, 17, 19, 22, 24, 65, 77, 131

zone, *see* comfort, learning

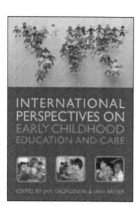

INTERNATIONAL PERSPECTIVES ON EARLY
CHILDHOOD EDUCATION AND CARE

Jan Georgeson and Jane Payler (Eds)

9780335245918 (Paperback)
February 2013

eBook also available

There is a growing interest in understanding how early years care and education is
organised and experienced internationally. This book examines key influential
approaches to early years care as well as some less well-known systems from
around the world.

Key features:

- Informs those studying early years about perspectives in other countries
- Encourages critical thinking about issues, influences and the
  complexities of early years provision around the world
- Promotes critical reflection on students' own provision and the current
  context of that provision

www.openup.co.uk

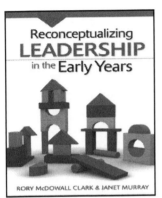

RECONCEPTUALIZING LEADERSHIP IN THE EARLY YEARS

Rory McDowall Clark and Janet Murray

9780335246243 (Paperback)
August 2012

eBook also available

This book explores the realities of leadership in the early years and examines the challenges and opportunities for the profession. The authors suggest that recent moves to professionalize the workforce offer a unique opportunity to reconceptualize leadership and develop a new paradigm more suited to the specific circumstances of the sector.

Key features:

- Ideas based on research from a wide range of current early years practice
- Real leadership profiles of practitioners from a diversity of different professional backgrounds and working in a variety of contexts
- Reflective prompts to assist you in identifying the leadership in your own practice and how this can be developed further

www.openup.co.uk

EARLY YEARS FOUNDATIONS
Critical Issues
Second Edition

Janet Moyles, Jane Payler & Jan Georgeson (Eds)

9780335262649 (Paperback)
February 2014

eBook also available

Among the many challenges facing early years professionals, there are continual
dilemmas arising between perceptions of good practice, the practicalities of provision
and meeting of STED requirements. This exciting and innovative new edition supports
practitioners in thinking through their responsibilities in tackling some of the many
challenges they encounter, for example, that children are still perceived as 'deficit' in
some way and in need of 'being school ready' rather than as developing individuals
who have a right to a childhood and appropriate early education.

Key features:

- Pedagogy
- Working with parents
- Difference and diversity

www.openup.co.uk

OPEN UNIVERSITY PRESS
McGraw - Hill Education

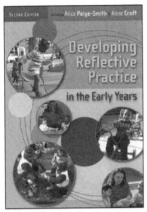

DEVELOPING REFLECTIVE PRACTICE IN THE EARLY YEARS 2/E

Alice Paige-Smith & Anna Craft

9780335242351 (Paperback)
2011

eBook also available

This book supports early years' practitioners in articulating and understanding their own practice in greater depth, exploring ways in which they can be encouraged to engage in reflecting on their practice.

The authors introduce ideas around creativity, inclusion, children's well being, partnership with parents and multidisciplinary team working, which will enable you to develop and explore the role of the early years' practitioner in further detail.

Key features of the book include:

- Updated and revised throughout to reflect latest policy changes and documents
- The role of the early years professional Reference to Children's Plan and Common Core of Skills and Knowledge for Children's Work Force
- New reflective questions and extended case studies
- Reference to safeguarding and child protection through joint-working

www.openup.co.uk

Printed in Great Britain
by Amazon